Good News

God Speaks to Mothers and Daughters

Dr. Bessie Flectcher, Ph.D.

LAEL PUBLISHING

GOOD NEWS! God Speaks to Mothers and Daughters
by Dr. Bessie S. Fletcher, Ph.D.
Editor: Georgina Chong-You
Published by Lael Publishing, LLC
Winston Salem, North Carolina
www.LaelPublishing.com

No part of this book may be used or reproduced in any form, stored in a retrieval system, or transmitted in any form by any means, electronic, photocopy, mechanical, recording or otherwise without written permission from the author. The only exception is for critical articles or reviews, in which brief excepts may be used.

ISBN 978-0-9916515-5-9

Copyright © 2016 by Dr. Bessie S. Fletcher
All Rights Reserved

Cover Designer and Design Director:
Angela Singletary Huntley

For more information visit the author's websites:
www.MDBN.org
www.DrBessieFletcher.org

First Edition

Printed in the United States of America.

Dedication

I dedicate this book to God our Father, Jesus Christ our Lord, and the Holy Spirit, and to my daughter, Angela, my son-in-law, Fella, my grandsons, Jared and Joshua, and my beloved family and friends.

Special Thanks to the Mother and Daughter Faith Trust Ministries staff and associates:

Education Director, Cynthia Oliver

Youth Director, N. Freeda Hunter

Photography and Video Director, Studio 104 Production, Paul Murray

Photographer, Janice Pauldo

Cover Picture by:
J's Photography, Janice Pauldo
Atlanta, Ga

Set arrangement by, Dorothy Westbrook

Reference Bibles: King James (KJ), New King James (NKJ) and English Standard Version (ESV)

Gifted with Love

Date: _____

To my Mother: _____

From your Daughter: _____

Or

To my Daughter: _____

From your Mother: _____

Comments:
_____
_____
_____
_____
_____

Contents

Introduction: The Purpose of This Book
Chapter One..**19**
Salvation for Mothers and Daughters
- The Prayer of Salvation
- The Importance of God's Word
- The Bible
- God's Promises to Mothers and Daughters
- The Gospels

Chapter Two..**31**
God's Compassion for Mothers and Daughters
- A Mother's Faith
- A Daughter's Faith
- When Mothers and Daughters Pray

Chapter Three..**49**
The Love of a Mother and Daughter

Chapter Four..**53**
God's Good Pleasure for Mothers and Daughters

Chapter Five...**57**
Your Body is not Your Own

Chapter Six...**67**
God Specially Selects Mothers and Daughters .

Chapter Seven..81
Wisdom for Mothers and Daughters
- Wisdom for Mothers
- Wisdom for Daughters
- Wisdom for Motherless Daughters
- Wisdom for Grandmothers
- Wisdom for Mothers-In-Law and Daughters-In-Law
- Wisdom for Barren and Childless Women
- God's Advice for Daughters
- A Daughter's Thanks to God

Chapter Eight..95
"The Standard" — For Both Mothers and Daughters

Chapter Nine..99
Congratulations Mother, It's a Girl!
- A Few Thoughts On Life Itself
- Food for Mothers and Daughters
- A Mother and Daughter's Best Life Now!

Chapter Ten..111
A Mother and Daughter's "Ultimate Weapon."
- The Power of a Mother's Word
- The Importance of Our Thoughts
- The Importance of Our Visions
- The Reality of Truth

Chapter Eleven..131
Mothers and Daughters: The Complete Package
- Mother and Daughter Health

- Mother and Daughter Peace
- Mother and Daughter Protection
- Mother and Daughter Joy
- Mother and Daughter Forgiveness
- Mother and Daughter Prosperity
- Mother and Daughter Wealth

Chapter Twelve..**151**

In Conclusion
- Mother and Daughter Bible Stories
- A Mother's Cry
- A Mother's Deadly Thoughts
- I Will Never Leave You
- From Orphan to Queen
- Mothers and Daughters Who Personally Interacted with Jesus
- A Good Mother Will Stand By Her Child's Side — To the Very End!
- Mother and Daughter Myrrh-Bearers for Jesus
- Mothers and Daughters at the Resurrection of Jesus
- Mothers and Daughters at the Ascension of Jesus
- Good News!
- Did You Know…?
- List of the Most Recognized Mothers and Daughters in the Bible
- Comprehensive List of Mothers and Daughters in the Bible

Introduction

The purpose of this book is to relay to the reader what God has to say about mothers and daughters, to mothers and daughters.

So, let's just start from the beginning!

In the beginning, God created the heavens and the earth. (Genesis 1:1)

God saw everything that He had made, and, behold it was very good! As days went by, God said to them, "Let us make man in our image." Then God made the man, and called him "Adam." That brought us to the sixth day. (Genesis 1: 26-31)

And on the seventh day God ended his work which he had done, and he rested on the seventh day from all his work which he had done. Then God blessed the seventh day and sanctified it because, in it, He rested from all His work which God had created and made. (Genesis 2:2-3)

Next, God looked around the heaven and earth, and When no bush of the field was yet in the land and no small plant of the field had yet sprung up — for the LORD God had not caused it to rain on the land, and there was no man to work the ground, and a mist was going up from the land and was watering the whole face of the ground... (Genesis 2:5-6)

Seeing that the grounds needed someone to till them, to

care for the plants and herbs, God realized He needed to create a man. Then the LORD God formed the man of dust from the ground and breathed into his nostrils the breath of life, and the man became a living creature. (Genesis 2:7)

Adam was the first created man. He was made and fashioned by God, in His image. Adam became God's first son!

And, Then the LORD God said, "It is not good that the man should be alone; I will make him a helper fit for him." (Genesis 2:18)

So the LORD God caused a deep sleep to fall upon the man, and while he slept took one of his ribs and closed up its place with flesh. And the rib that the LORD God had taken from the man he made into a woman and brought her to the man. (Genesis 2:21-22)

And Adam said, "…This at last is bone of my bones and flesh of my flesh; she shall be called Woman because she was taken out of Man." (Genesis 2:23)

Eve was the first created woman. God's first daughter! As I see it, Eve was the daughter of the Lord God. She was designed to be the wife of Adam.

To many, the creation of the first man and woman is a familiar story, including the part where Adam and Eve came together, Eve became pregnant with their first son, Cain, and at his birth, she became the World's Very First Mother. Eve was the model and image for women for many generations after. The Bible offers us the stories and histories of many women

Introduction

throughout generations. All of these women were someone's daughter, obviously, and the majority of them filled the role of mother, as well. And Eve, once again, as the world's very first daughter and mother, serves as a model for us all.

At the same time, though we read about many different women in the scriptures, we don't find too many references to actual mothers and daughters in the Bible. If you were to ask someone who's pretty familiar with the Word of God, "Can you name some mother-daughter stories in the Bible?" most would not be able to tell you quickly. Some would likely mention Naomi and Ruth, but these two women were not a true mother and daughter…they were mother-in-law and daughter-in-law, and the difference matters, as we'll find out later.

Take a moment to ask yourself the same question now: Can I name some mother-daughter stories in the Bible?

Most likely, you won't come up with too many. Which brings me to the reason God inspired me to write this book: Because He wants you to know that He loves you, Mother, and He loves you, Daughter, and He didn't leave you out! He loves you individually — whether you're a daughter only, and you're not a mother, or you happen to fill both roles — and He loves you collectively. The bottom line is God truly cares about the mother-daughter relationship. And that's Good News!

So, as you read this book, keep in mind that through it, God is extending to you His precious thoughts on how important mothers and daughters are, and how their roles factor into His divine will and plan. He wants you to know that He loves you so much, He chose you, Mother, to carry a portion of His Spirit in the earth realm, in the form of that being the precious daughter He's entrusted into your care!

The role of the mother is so important; in fact, my belief is that when the spirit of an unconceived, unborn daughter leaves the Spirit of God, it enters the mother directly from God. That's why it's so vitally important that mothers do their very best to nurture their daughters carefully, even before they are born, during the nine months they're being shaped in the womb. As a woman, you are playing either the role of a daughter, or the dual role of a mother-daughter. Not all women are mothers, but all are certainly someone's daughter — even if their parents are deceased. The point is, if you're a woman, through this book, God has something important to say to you about one or more of your most important roles in life!

If someone were to walk up to you and tell you, "Hey, God wants to speak to you!", What would your initial thoughts be? I know it sounds like a strange scenario, but would you think:

- Speak to me about what?
- Did I do something wrong?
- Are you sure you're talking to the right person?
- I had no idea God would bother speaking to someone like me!

Whatever your responding thoughts would be, guess

Introduction

what? God is always speaking to you! And He's waiting for you to speak back to Him, through your intra-conversations (those ongoing conversations within your head), prayer, and the intimate communication that characterizes your personal relationship with God.

God is not human. He has no emotions. God is Pure Love, and that love enables Him to love you unconditionally. There is nothing that you could do, say, or think, in other words, to cause permanent separation between you and God. Nothing! How do I know? Because those intra-conversations, which are going on inside your head, even right now, never cease between you and God.

Right now in my spirit, I hear the Lord saying, "Mother, you are my Eve! And you are my Eve, too, Daughter!" That is a Rhema word (defined as the spoken Word of God, applicable to a current situation or need for direction) to be thoughtfully pondered and meditated!

As you read this book, understand that God is speaking to you out of love, and not from a place of wanting to condemn you. Rather, He wants to remind you of why He created you in the first place, and if you aren't already familiar, I want to inform you of the new covenant He has made available for you, through His Son, Jesus Christ.

God is unhappy about the high numbers of mothers and daughters who don't know about His new covenant, as revealed to us through the gospel, which is "the good news." Sound familiar?

Also, through this book, God is sending you a reminder of yet another aspect of His Good News, for those of you who've never heard or received the gospel of Jesus Christ, which He brought straight down from God in heaven to humanity, you are in for one mind-opening, soul-renewing experience! The real "good news" will truly change the way you think and speak, as well as the way you see and experience life. So, if you're ready for a brand-new life-experience, one that leads to salvation, good health, wealth, and prosperity. Do yourself a favor and READ ON!

Chapter One

Salvation for Mothers and Daughters

Salvation is a personal relationship with Jesus Christ. To receive it, you simply must make the decision to invite Jesus, who is LOVE, to come live in your heart. You do this by first repenting of your sins, then asking God's forgiveness for them, and finally, praying the prayer of salvation.

God sacrificed His Son, Jesus, for us, so that we could have a direct relationship with God Himself. This way, we would get to experience His love for us, be forgiven of our sins, live free from sin and fear, live a life of peace, experience healing and prosperity, and live an overall joyous life! Jesus died, in other words, so that we might live. And the number-one motivating force behind this act of ultimate self-sacrifice on His part was nothing less than His extreme LOVE for us!

When we put God first in our lives, we begin to live the

life He designed specifically for us. In fact, if you aren't already living that life, you can start right now, right where you are. You can do something right now, while you're reading, that will enable you to start enjoying the incredible blessings and promises of God!

Here's what you do…

First, take three deep breaths. That will help you begin to clear your mind, in preparation for your new life in Christ.

Next, you need to acknowledge to both yourself and God that you're a sinner. Now, repent of your sins. To repent means to have a changed mind about your actions; to have sincere regret about one's wrongdoing or sins; to make a commitment to doing wrong no more!

Next, Believe on the Lord Jesus Christ, and you shall be saved, and your house. (Acts 16:31) Scripture tells us, *"He who believeth on the Son has everlasting life: and he that believeth not the Son shall not see life; but the wrath of God abideth on him."* (John 3:36)!

The final way to activate this process called salvation is through a prayer. So, all you have to do now is say the Prayer of Salvation aloud, while believing in your heart that what you are saying is true. And that's it — once you do so, you are SAVED!

The Prayer of Salvation
Father God,

I recognize and acknowledge that I am a sinner. I am sorry for my actions, for I know they have displeased You, and I ask now that You forgive my sins. I believe that Jesus Christ died on the cross for me, and then He rose from the dead! I, therefore, confess Jesus Christ as my Lord and Savior, and I make Him Lord of my life today. Jesus, I invite you into my heart to live and to guide me for the rest of my life. I believe that I am saved according to your Word, and this confession of faith. In Your precious name. Amen!

If you prayed this prayer of salvation and believed in your heart the words that you spoke, you are indeed SAVED! You also need to know that you are now "covered by the blood of Jesus." Essentially this means that He is both protecting you and guiding you as you begin living a life of holiness that pleases Him.

Congratulations, Reader, and welcome to the Christian family, the Body of Christ!

The Importance of God's Word

A wondering or frustrated mother might exclaim, "Wow if only there were an instruction book on how to properly raise a daughter!" And, God would say in response, *"Ask, and it shall be given you; Seek, and ye shall find; Knock, and it shall be opened unto you." (Matthew 7:7)*

In other words, God is letting us know, Mothers, You need to consult the ultimate book. Your answers are in The Holy Bible!

You'd be truly amazed at some of the godly advice and instructions that come straight from the Word of God to mothers and daughters, specifically — IF they would only bother to look there!

Once again, this book was written to inspire and encourage you to seek out what God has to say to you as a mother, and as a daughter. It reveals many of His thoughts, truths, standards, and expectations of us mothers and daughters, as well as His Will concerning mother-daughter relationships.

BIBLE

Basic **I**nformation **B**efore **L**eaving **E**arth

The Holy Bible is the greatest book ever written. Some creative person even came up with a wonderful little acronym that best sums up its value and purpose to us all. The words "B.I.B.L.E.", they said, stands for "Basic Information Before Leaving Earth". Isn't that clever? Then, someone else gave it an even more accurate definition: "Basic Instructions Before Leaving Earth".

I say instructions is a more fitting word. Sometimes we seem to forget that the Bible contains God's actual guidelines and commands for our lives and that its purpose is actually to instruct us, as opposed to inform us.

Regarding information, though, the Bible is comprised of sixty-six books, written by about forty different authors. It's divided into two testaments, the Old Testament and the New Testament. It was said that Paul the Apostle wrote nearly two-thirds of the New Testament.

Furthermore, the Bible, also known as "God's Word," is written out in the form of stories, historical references, prophecies, instructions, commands, consequences, and — very importantly, too — promises to His dear children.

God's promises to those who carefully follow His instructions on how to live this life says this, in a nutshell: If you do this, you can expect Me to do that amazing thing for you in return! In other words, do as I say, and I will do what I said!

God's Word reveals His will for humanity, and for the most part, it is clear, direct, straight, and to-the-point. The decision of whether or not to act on it and obey it is always up to you, the hearer. And the results you get from whatever daily decisions you make concerning God's Word is what makes up your total life experience!

The Bible contains God's recipe for success. In other words, if you follow it precisely, you get its promised results. And those results are always good. If you find in your life that you're not *"eating the good of the land" (Isaiah 1:19)*, as the Word says, you may just want to evaluate the life-recipe that you happen to be following. To see what "ingredients" might be missing! You don't have to be a chef to know that every properly repeated recipe will produce whatever dish it promises!

Bottom line, the Bible is the ultimate resource for Christian living. It contains God's actual words — both those He spoke and those He inspired men's minds and hands to write down — of ultimate wisdom and guidance for your life. And whenever God's words are properly regarded and applied, they lead to change — to the occurrence of miracles in your life.

And of course, Mothers, once you learn for yourself the "basic instructions" found in the Bible, the Word of God, don't hesitate or neglect to teach them to your daughters!

God's Promises to Mothers and Daughters

As mentioned earlier, salvation is a personal decision to accept Jesus Christ as Lord and Savior. Unfortunately, most of us don't begin to even think about Jesus, until something bad happens in our lives to make us suddenly desperate for His help or protection!

That's just the way it is with human beings sometimes. It's only when we're sick and tired of our present condition that we finally begin to search for real answers to seek guidance from our higher source. Certain situations in life just have a way of making you cry out, "Lord, HELP me!"

For example, those of you mothers who are single and filling the role of "head of the household" may find yourselves crying out desperately at times, as you work hard to provide for your children on too little income while struggling to rear them properly. At the end of a long, hard day, when the kids are all in bed, and you finally have a moment to be alone with your thoughts, you may end up asking yourself, "How in the world did I end up here?"

But if you're a Christian with a genuine relationship with God, you will hear inside yourself the gentle reply of a still, small voice. It assures you saying, "Don't worry, I am here. I am with you, and I understand. Let Me help you."

Sometimes, even when you have that relationship with God, you may choose to seek out the wisdom and advice of an older woman — your mother, your grandmother, or a neighbor, perhaps. Once you've shared with her all that you're going through, and explained the endless challenges you're facing as a single parent, if she's a believer herself, she'll likely wind up telling you what you already know in your heart. "Baby, you need to take it to the Lord in prayer. Just let Him work it out!"

The point here is that we sometimes need other believers to remind us of our two greatest resources as Christians: Prayer and the Promises! That's partly what this book is here to do.

Part of your "salvation package" is the manifested promises of God in your life. Realize this, learn what you're entitled to; believe what He said, and lay claim on what's already yours! Here are just a few of your exceptional "benefits"!

"And my God shall supply all your need according to his riches in glory by Christ Jesus." (Philippians 4:19)

"...By which he has granted to us his precious and very great promises so that through them you may become partakers of the divine nature, having escaped from the corruption that is in the world because of sinful desire." (2 Peter 1:4)

"For all the promises of God in Him are Yes, and in Him Amen, unto the glory of God through us." (II Corinthians 1:20)

"I can do all things through Christ who strengthens me." (Philippians 4:13)

"In hope of eternal life, which God, who cannot lie, promised before the world began..." (Titus 1:2)

"For the LORD God is a sun and shield; the LORD bestows favor and honor. No good thing does he withhold from those who walk uprightly." (Psalms 84:11)

"I will not leave you as orphans; I will come to you." (John 14:18)

"Since we have these promises, beloved, let us cleanse ourselves from every defilement of body and spirit, bringing holiness to completion in the fear of God." (2 Corinthians 7:1)

The Gospels

The gospels are "the good news" about why Jesus came to the earth. They are the stories and teachings of Jesus Christ Himself, as recorded by four of the men, called disciples, who knew and followed Him.

The four gospels — Matthew, Mark, Luke, and John — make up the first four books of the New Testament and within their texts are words spoken by Jesus Himself. Some versions of the Bible even have Jesus' words highlighted in red, so that they're unmistakable to the reader. But even Jesus' spoken words were God-inspired, because according to Jesus, He only did what His Father, who is God, told Him to do (John 12:49). This guiding principle that He lived by — only to say and do what the Father says and instructs — is enough by itself to get us from here to heaven if we follow Jesus' example and live by it!

Here's a sampling of some of the most profound scriptures found in the Gospels:

"...And saying, "The time is fulfilled, and the kingdom of God is at hand; repent and believe in the gospel." (Mark 1:15)

"And Jesus went about all Galilee, teaching in their synagogues, preaching the gospel of the kingdom, and healing all kinds of sickness and all kinds of disease among the people." (Matthew 4:23)

"The blind see and the lame walk; the lepers are cleansed, and the deaf hears; the dead are raised up, and the poor have the gospel preached to them." (Matthew 11:5)

"And He said to them, 'Go into all the world and preach the gospel to every creature.'" (Mark 16:15)

"And this gospel of the kingdom will be preached in all the world as a witness to all the nations, and then the end will come. "(Matthew 24:14)

Jesus was sent into the world to teach and preach the

gospel. He, therefore, traveled throughout the cities, villages, and synagogues of His region, preaching that "the Kingdom of God was at hand" — which meant that the time for God to reign and rule in the earth is now!

Mothers and Daughters, what Jesus was also giving to the world, both then and now, was a warning: He was advising us to have faith in what He was saying and to repent, or the consequences would be harsh and irreversible!

As we said before, Jesus was also quick to let His hearers know He was only repeating the words of His Father. He essentially was delivering a message that didn't originate with Him, but that came from the God of all creation.

In like manner, Mothers, God is telling you to repent, and to get your household and family in order, if you haven't already. If you don't, the consequences will be dire! The time is near, and, once again, it's now!

In the end, the Kingdom of God is the only true hope for the entire world, which obviously includes mothers and daughters. So then, Mothers and Daughters, as you read the Word of God for yourself, realize that you will find many of your answers within the gospels themselves — answers that lead to your healing, to your prosperity, and to peace, love, and joy in your mother-daughter relationship!

Chapter Two

God's Compassion for Mothers and Daughters

Here's some more Good News for mothers and their daughters: God has compassion for the mother-daughter relationship. No matter what state or condition your relationship is in, be encouraged to know that you can turn it around!

And I mean you can turn it around NOW! You do this by repenting, and saying only the Words of God that represent your vision of an ideal mother-daughter relationship.

God will honor your will, as long as it lines up with His. His Will allows you to start all over again, and simply create a whole new dynamic — one that is positive and pleasing to God — in your mother-daughter relationship!

How do you start all over again? Well, again, you start by creating a relationship with Jesus Christ, making him your Lord and Savior. Once you've done that, keep reading, and allow God to reveal the answers to all your mother-daughter concerns.

Pay close attention to Mark 11:22, where Jesus gave this strong hint: *"Have faith in God."*

In another New Testament passage, John 2:1-5, you'll find a similarly powerful suggestion from Jesus' mother, Mary.

On the third day, there was a wedding at Cana in Galilee, and the mother of Jesus was there. Jesus also was invited to the wedding with his disciples.

When the wine ran out, the mother of Jesus said to him, *"They have no wine."* And Jesus said to her, *"Woman, what does this have to do with me? My hour has not yet come."*

His mother said to the servants, *"Do whatever he tells you." (John 2:1-5)*

Let me rephrase for you what Mother Mary was essentially trying to tell us:

Whatever Jesus asks you to do, just to do it!

To start all over again in your mother-daughter relationship, He asks you to repent of your sins, and go and sin no more.

Remember the accused woman of adultery?

The scribes and the Pharisees brought a woman who had been caught in adultery, and placing her in the midst; they said to him, *"Teacher, this woman has been caught in the act of adultery.*

Now in the Law Moses commanded us to stone such women. So what do you say?" This they said to test him, that they might have some charge to bring against him. Jesus bent down and wrote with his finger on the ground.

And as they continued to ask him, he stood up and said to them, *"Let him who is without sin among you be the first to throw a stone at her."* And once more he bent down and wrote on the ground. But when they heard it, they went away one by one, beginning with the older ones, and Jesus was left alone with the woman standing before him.

Jesus stood up and said to her, *"Woman, where are they? Has no one condemned you?"* She said, *"No one, Lord."* And Jesus said, *"Neither do I condemn you; go, and from now on sin no more." (John 8:3-11)*

The woman immediately decided to sin no more, and it turned her entire life around. She was able to start all over again! No matter what you have done, what you have said, or even what you haven't done or haven't said, God will forgive you and allow you to begin again!

God sent Jesus to both declare and demonstrate to you how much He loves you, just the way you are, and He wants you to know He is quick to forgive you and remember your sins no more!

So at this point, you are born again and removed from your sins. You are now sin-free!

In other words, God just resets you. Isn't that some truly Good News?

Mother, when your daughter sees that you are changing your ways and living a godly lifestyle, it fulfills the will of God and pleases Him. You are the role model for your daughter, after all; she is watching you. She hears and sees your actions on a daily basis. She knows when you tell the truth, and she also knows when you tell a lie. Your daughter is affected and "trained" by the very actions you take, and she is affected by those same spirits affecting you.

That's why God says, *"As is the Mother, so is her Daughter." (Ezekiel 16:44)*

This word from God means that your words, thoughts, and feelings, Mother, affects the words, thoughts, and feelings of your daughter.

Mothers, this is why it is so very important that you watch what you say in the presence of your daughter because those words will not return void! One day, Mother, you will find yourself listening to words and hearing thoughts and feelings that are your creation, but they will be coming from the mouth of your teenage daughter! You'll be thinking, incredulously, "Where in the world does she get the nerve to speak to me that way, in that tone of voice?"

Again, *"As is the Mother, so is her Daughter." (Ezekiel 16:44)*

In other words, she gets it from you!

It's amazing how powerful those words are when you take a few minutes to think on them.

One day, as I was walking from one room to the other in my home, I heard the voice of God clearly ask me, "Would you like to know what I think about mothers and daughters?"

I stopped in my tracks, turned my head to the left, looked back over my shoulder, and said, "Well, yes!"

That's when He led me to Ezekiel 16:44, and the eight profound words He wanted me to focus on: *"As is the Mother, so is her Daughter."*

I couldn't help but reply to Him, "God, you've had me working with mothers and daughters for nearly twelve years. Why are you just now telling me this?"

And God said, "You didn't need to know it until now!"

At that time, I had been working with mothers and their daughters (and other family members) for twelve years, as a Christian clinical psychologist. I've now been doing Christian mother-daughter counseling, crusades, bonding workshops, conferences, appreciation events, galas and cruises, all centered on mothers and their daughters, for the past fifteen years.

As I continued to meditate on Ezekiel 16:44, I started to reflect back in my mind through the many conversations and counseling sessions I'd held with my mother-daughter clients. How many times had I heard a daughter emphatically state, "I do not want to be like my mother!"

Deep inside me, a small voice would say in reply,

"Really! Just keep living." But I would only smile.

You may have said those same words, yourself: "I am NOT going to be like my mother!" But as you continued to grow and then have a family of your own, you no doubt realized that so much of what you say and do are the same things, as what your mother used to say and do!

Somehow, the very things you said you'd never repeat to your children, or do concerning them, found their way into your mouth and your actions. Wow! Powerful, isn't it?

Now, I know that not every daughter feels this way. Some daughters are a bit clearer in their determinations of what they like and don't like about their mothers, and what they don't intend to repeat. Based on my years of mother and daughter counseling, I would guess that nine out of ten daughters have a specific area of disagreement with her mother's rearing process.

The daughters surely are convinced that they have a better way than their mother's of handling certain situations. They feel that they would improve on her technique, if in a similar situation with their daughter. Still, when their turn comes around, they typically discover that rearing a daughter is not as easy as they thought!

So now the daughter finds herself reverting to what were her mother's parenting skills, though she may sometimes be successful in bringing a new twist to the mothering old techniques.

As the daughter who is now a mother endeavors to take

mothering to a new-and-improved level, she may just end up giving in and declaring what I've heard many young mothers say: "Oh, well — the way my mother reared me obviously worked, since I didn't turn out so bad!"

God also brought to my attention that the mother is the first point of contact to the daughter, once her spirit leaves Him in heaven. That means that the mother holds the second-greatest power of influence after God over the spirit of her daughter, and that's even before she is born.

All thoughts, emotions, words, visions, touches, impressions and expressions that the mother experiences on earth, the daughter also feels and experiences, inside the womb.

Now, this is where it gets deep...

God also spoke to me and said, "Whenever a mother enters a sinful environment, though she may think it's her secret and no one will ever know. Those sinful spirits inevitably attach themselves to her, and once she goes back into her living environment, those sinful spirits attach themselves to the spirit of her daughter!"

In many of my counseling sessions, I've brought to the attention of the mother that her daughter is just like her!

As I listen to my various clients share their life experiences, they inevitably tell me what some of their mother's experiences were, and it's like they're looking directly in a mirror. Like mother, like daughter, in other words!

Sounds familiar, right?

Sounds a lot like Ezekiel 16:44, doesn't it? *"As is the Mother, so is her Daughter."*

Why am I sharing this with you? Because the knowledge of it plays an important role in helping the mother realize that when she cleans up her spiritual act, she cleans up her daughter's spiritual act, as well — even if her daughter doesn't recognize or acknowledge it.

You also need to know, Mother, that the same way you brought those negative spirits into your daughter's life, you have the ability to cancel them out!

Don't wait until your daughter becomes mature and starts to enter her pre-teen and teenage years, when negative spirits start to act out and eventually become uncontrollable! When that happens, you'll find yourself crying out, "I don't know what happened to that girl!" Rather, take control now by reading the Word and seeking God's guidance. Do it now, before it's too late!

I can't tell you how many times I've witnessed in my mother-daughter relationship workshops a great-grandmother, grandmother, mother, and daughter — that's four generations — all living the same negative mindset and lifestyle!

Whenever I see this, it's clear to me that it's nothing but the effects of a generational curse!

Someone has to stop the generational curse in your family. Why shouldn't it be you?

Mothers, God is holding you accountable for the outcome

of your daughters; they are, in truth, His daughters. Still, He's holding you accountable and responsible for them, and you have the power to stop any generational curses that are operating in your family, right now, simply by "Renewing Your Mind."

Jesus Christ has saved you from all negative spirits, as well as the curse of the law!

Christ redeemed us from the curse of the law by becoming a curse for us — for it is written, *"Cursed is everyone who is hanged on a tree"— (Galatians 3:13)*

To "hang on a tree" is to live as the world lives: under a curse.

To live as one who is redeemed, on the other hand, is to live as Jesus has instructed us: by the Word of God!

"God is not a man, that he should lie, or a son of man, that he should change his mind. Has he said, and will he not do it? Or has he spoken, and will he not fulfill it?" (Numbers 23:19)

"Therefore I tell you, whatever you ask in prayer, believe that you have received it, and it will be yours." (Mark 11:24)

Mark 11: 22, 23 and 24 are three Bible verses I regularly use to build my faith. I read them in the morning, I meditate on them throughout the day, and then I read them at night, before going to bed.

God is not a man that He should lie (Numbers 23:19), the Word says. And if He doesn't lie, then it means He always tells the truth!

"And you shall know the truth, and the truth shall make

you free." (John 8:32)

The truth will make you free from sin, sickness, poverty, fear, doubt, lack, stress, shame, unforgiveness, depression, and loneliness.

Mothers, once you believe, teach this same Good News to your daughters! That is how you help raise up a whole new generation of believers for the Kingdom of God!

Remember Mothers: you are the first point of contact for your daughters after they've left their original heavenly home with God and before they enter the natural world!

When we put God first in our lives, we begin to live the life He designed specifically for us. In fact, if you aren't already living that life, you can start right now, right where you are.

God trusts you! Now ask yourself if you trust God?

A mother may respond honestly, "Well, I want to trust God, but I sometimes get confused as to what it means actually to trust Him and have faith."

God's Word says, "*Now faith is the substance of things hoped for, the evidence of things not seen.*" *(Hebrews 11:1)*

So Jesus answered and said to them, "*Have faith in God.*" *(Mark 11:22)*

"*Truly, I say to you, whoever says to this mountain, 'Be taken up and thrown into the sea,' and does not doubt in his heart, but believes that what he says will come to pass, it will be done for him.*" *(Mark 11:23)*

"*Therefore I tell you, whatever you ask in prayer, believe that you have received it, and it will be yours.*" *(Mark 11:24)*

"*For we walk by faith, not by sight.*" *(2 Corinthians 5:7)*

In answer to this mother's query about what it means to have faith, I would tell her, Faith is trusting wholeheartedly in God! You can't trust God if you don't believe in Him. Faith believes that every word God has spoken is absolutely, unquestionably true!

If you believe that statement, then you trust God!

A Mother's Faith

When sickness attacks a mother's daughter, she will find someone to help her with her faith and trust issues. But first and foremost, her first thoughts should be to call on the name of Jesus!

She may take her daughter to a hospital to get professional medical help, but in the meantime, she should also be seeking the Word of God and praying, as well as soliciting the prayers of those she knows has a strong intimate relationship with God, such as her mother, grandmother, or her Pastor. But once a mother recognizes that her help for healing comes from only one Source, the Blood of Jesus, all she needs then is a witness. God said,

"Again I say to you that if two of you shall agree on earth concerning anything that they ask, it will be done for them by My Father in heaven. For where two or three are gathered together in My name, I am there in the midst of them." (Matthew 18:19-20)

"And behold, a woman of Canaan came from that region and cried out to Him, saying, "Have mercy on me, O Lord, Son of David! My daughter is severely demon-possessed."

"But He answered her not a word. And His disciples came and urged Him, saying, "Send her away, for she cries out after us." But He answered and said, "I was not sent except to the lost sheep of the house of Israel." Then she came and worshiped Him, saying, "Lord, help me!" (Matthew15:22-25)

Prayer and worship, along with your faith, will move God to act on your behalf!

"Then Jesus answered and said to her, "O woman, great is your faith! Let it be to you as you desire. And her daughter was healed from that very hour." (Matthew 15:28)

A Daughter's Faith

Daughters, you have to seek God for yourself! It can also help, too, to have a prayer partner.

I would advise you in your selection of a prayer partner to make sure you see and feel the Spirit of God within them. Just having a prayer partner doesn't ensure you'll get an answer to your prayer. What you have to do is operate according to Scripture, which says that the two of you must agree on His Word for that particular situation.

"Again I say to you, If two of you agree on earth about anything they ask, it will be done for them by my Father in heaven. For where two or three are gathered in my name, there am I among them." (Matthew 18:19-20)

The point here is that the two of you have to *agree in spirit*.

Suppose you are looking for a prayer partner to agree with you, and you find someone you believe is qualified, but in the middle of praying, you sense that the two of you are not agreeing in spirit. That's when you realize that the two of you are not following the Word of God, and you've now got to find someone else who meets the spiritual qualifications.

Or, let's say you ask your prayer partner to pray for you about something in particular, and she simply says, "I will." Is that a real agreement?

As a Bible-believing mother or daughter, you may understand that your prayer partner has good intentions, but it's not good intentions that move God. So sometimes, you have to take matters into your hands. Which reminds me of a particular daughter in the Bible who did just that. Hers was a situation all mothers and daughters can relate to, too!

Mothers and daughters, you know what it's like to experience your menstrual cycle, or "period," every month? Some months can be worse than others, right? But try to imagine what it would be like to have a period *every day*, for *twelve long years straight*. That is an unimaginable, nearly tragic scenario to process, in your mind?

I can only imagine what might've gone through the mind of this daughter "with the issue of blood," as the Bible says about her, having such an unusually long menstrual cycle! I guess, too, that given the unstoppable blood-flow that she suffered, she probably sought out early for a prayer partner. Either way, her situation did not improved; she only continued to lose blood. Finally, in her twelfth year of sickness, she heard about Jesus' coming through town.

This daughter had built her faith to a point where she was able to make the firm decision, "I'm going to get close enough to Jesus to touch the hem of his garment, and I know that I will be healed!"

"And behold, a woman who had suffered from a discharge of blood for twelve years came up behind him and touched the fringe of his garment, for she said to herself, "If I only touch his garment, I will be made well." (Matthew 9:20-21)

This daughter succeeded in getting close enough to touch the hem of Jesus' garment. Once she did, she waited nervously for His response!

"Jesus turned, and seeing her; he said, 'Take heart, daughter; your faith has made you well.' And instantly the woman was made well." (Matthew 9:22)

When Mothers and Daughters Pray

Mothers and Daughters, God wants you to know that when you pray, you don't have to do so for hours, saying the same words over and over again! His word says,

"And when you pray, you must not be like the hypocrites. For they love to stand and pray in the synagogues and at the street corners, that they may be seen by others. Truly, I say to you, they have received their reward." (Matthew 6:5)

Repetition of words doesn't impress God at all.
Doing what He asks you to do impresses Him!
His Word tells us to make our requests known unto Him

by asking for what we want, in the name of Jesus Christ. Once we ask, we simply need to believe that He will do what He said, and then we can thank Him with faith — ahead of time!

Now you're free to move on to something else, as you consider what you just requested of God a "done deal"!

God's Word further tells us:

"Be anxious for nothing, but in everything by prayer and supplication, with thanksgiving, let your requests be made known to God..." (Philippians 4:6)

Your best place of prayer is a quiet area where you can be alone with God. He loves it when you spend quality time with Him. Making God feel special like this gets His attention!

"Therefore I say to you, whatever things you ask when you pray, believe that you receive them, and you will have them." (Mark 11:24)

If you don't know how to pray, or what to pray for, just ask God, as the disciples did:

"Now it came to pass, as He was praying in a certain place, when He ceased, that one of His disciples said to Him, "Lord, teach us to pray, as John also taught his disciples."

"So He said to them, 'When you pray, say:

"Our Father in heaven,
Hallowed be Your name.
Your kingdom come.
Your will be done
On earth as it is in heaven.
Give us day by day our daily bread.
And forgive us our sins,
For we also forgive everyone who is indebted to us.
And do not lead us into temptation,
But deliver us from the evil one.'" (Luke 11:2-4)

Chapter Three

The Love of a Mother and Daughter

God is a Spirit, and He is made up of 100% pure love! Pure love is spotless, uncontaminated, and innocent. It is love without fault or blame. Pure love is God Himself!

In fact, according to Scripture, *"Anyone who does not love does not know God, because God is love."* (I John 4:8)

Mothers, God expects you to love Him as He loves you. He also expects you to share His love. As He extends His love to you, He expects you to extend it to others — and that includes your daughters!

Of course, Mothers, you must first *know* the love of God, and how to love, to properly demonstrate love to your daughters.

Love is a spirit. It is expressed through one's words and actions. But to qualify as genuine love, it also must come from the heart. Because the Spirit cannot be seen or touched, the only methods we have of expressing and interpreting love is through words, actions, and spiritual discernment.

How can you demonstrate pure love?

Pure love is unconditional. You demonstrate it by your quickness to forgive, and also to be mindful of your words. Once you speak a Word, it's like firing a bullet from a gun; you can't stop it, and you can't take it back! It always hit its intended target, revealing its intentions!

So, Mothers, when you are speaking to your young daughters especially, you need to watch your words, as well as your tone of voice. One word wrapped up in the wrong tone can lead to misinterpretation and misunderstanding. That misinterpreted, misunderstood word can potentially create an impression in your daughter's mind that will negatively affect your mother-daughter relationship in the future!

As a Christian clinical psychologist, I've witnessed how misinterpreted words spoken between a mother and daughter can suddenly show up in a counseling session, some twenty or thirty years, later. In one memorable example, a daughter heard unloving words from her mother at the age of five. Those words that she heard led her to believe that her mother didn't love her, and she held onto that belief for a very long time… for decades!

Once a daughter comes to the conclusion that her mother doesn't love her, it affects her intra-conversations, energy, and her spirit. She doesn't want to be around her mother anymore. She spends less time with her, and shares very little with her.

She only says what is necessary, as she tells herself, about her mother's house, "I can't wait to get out of here!"

Because she didn't share her "true" thoughts and feelings with her mother, as a child, she had to deal with her intra-conversations all alone, without anyone to help interpret them. Intra-conversations that go unchecked can take on a life and form of their own! A daughter's intra-conversations, in most cases, when she's young, tell her things that are not true. Keep in mind, though, that the daughter is only seeing and hearing in reaction to the past negative words that she heard from her mother — she's interpreting from a place of not feeling loved!

Those negative words that helped formed the feelings and thoughts of not being loved became embedded in her daughter's subconscious mind. And those same words will resurface in the future to justify her decisions and actions.

This same situation will play a role in the daughter's decisions concerning her relationship with her mother, as well, and possibly affect her future relationship with her daughter, too.

The *Good News* is this: Change can start with forgiveness and a mere honest conversation, true love and respect. Honest discourse has the potential to redeem the time lost between a mother and daughter.

God sent Jesus to show us how to love each other. So whenever you feel you don't know how to properly or fully show your mother or daughter love, read the scriptures to find out what God has to say on the subject!

"For God so loved the world that He gave His only begotten Son, that whoever believes in Him should not perish but have everlasting life."*(John 3:16)*

"Love suffers long and is kind; love does not envy; love does not parade itself, is not puffed up… "*(I Corinthians 13:4)*

"But I say to you who hear: Love your enemies, do good to those who hate you, bless those who curse you, and pray for those who spitefully use you." (Luke 6:27-28)

"Beloved, let us love one another, for love is of God; and everyone who loves is born of God and knows God." (1 John 4:7)

"He who has My commandments and keeps them, it is he who loves Me. And he who loves Me will be loved by My Father, and I will love him and manifest Myself to him." (John 14:21)

Chapter Four

God's Good Pleasure for Mothers and Daughters

Pure love from a mother to her daughter will generate pure love from the daughter back to her mother, as the result! Every seed reproduces after its kind. We all know that an apple can't reproduce an orange, nor can corn develop from tomato seeds. That's impossible!

God's Word tells us He made man in His very own image, so this means that mothers and daughters are made in the image of God, too; and again, God is pure love. That means that mothers and daughters ought to deal with each other from a place of pure love, too, just like God!

Because love is not a tangible object, it must be measured through words, thoughts, and feelings. Feelings are an especially strong indicator of emotions, and love is no exception. If a person makes you feel good, you can conclude that they at least like you. When nice, kind words are added on top of those loving feelings, and a relationship continues to develop in a positive manner, we tend to label that bond *love*.

Now, one thing most of us humans tend to associate with the word "love" is food! If you were to ask someone what their favorite food is, the mere thought of the answer would very likely put a smile on their face, as they responded with delight, "I *love* my mother's cinnamon rolls!"

Again, in this example, the word "love" is being used in connection with something edible and perishable: food! Have you ever created a meal from a recipe, or even "from scratch," and the way it turned out made you feel all good inside? Remember how pleased you were from just looking at it, once you were finally done preparing it? Even more, remember the special pleasure you got from tasting it?

Speaking of taste, that reminds me of one of my most sought-after recipes — one that my family and friends often request. My peach cobbler!

When I make my peach cobbler, it gives me great pleasure to see that golden-brown crust topping over sweet peaches, simmering with the smells of cinnamon, nutmeg and lots of butter!

Sometimes after I've made it, I'll stand back and just look at it saying to myself, "That looks *good*!" And I get even greater pleasure when my family and friends tell me they enjoyed consuming it!

If our food gives us great pleasure, as both creators and partakers, can you imagine the extreme pleasure that God gets when we, His precious creations, do good things?

I can only imagine how proud God must have been after He created the first man and woman, as He watched them play like children in His beautiful Garden of Eden. We, human beings, are indeed the apple of our Creator's eye!

Then God said, "Let us make man in our image, after our likeness. And let them have dominion over the fish of the sea and over the birds of the heavens and over the livestock and over all the earth and over every creeping thing that creeps on the earth." (Genesis 1:26)

"And God saw everything that he had made, and behold, it was very good. And there was evening and there was morning, the sixth day." (Genesis 1:31)

God created us for His good pleasure, for His pure enjoyment! He wants to see us playing like little children, enjoying this big, incredible world He created just for us!

Yes, we are still in the "Garden of Eden," as we occupy this earth; this world is the same "earth garden" that Adam and Eva lived on at the dawn of humanity. Surprised? And just as He did then, God gets great pleasure when we enjoy, ask for, and receive of His many incredible blessings!

If you look back at the times when you received something you sincerely wanted as a child, you can probably recall jumping up and down, and even screaming and hollering with joy!

That something was a gift from God to you. Delivered to you by a man or a woman, such as your parents, but the Originator of that good thing you got, whatever it was, was from God. As the Word tells us:

"Every good gift and every perfect gift is from above, coming down from the Father of lights with whom there is no variation or shadow due to change." (James 1:17)

It also tells us to *"Ask, and it will be given to you; seek, and you will find; knock, and it will be opened to you." (Matthew 7:7)*

Chapter Five

Your Body is not Your Own

Whenever you create a thing, it's safe to say that you own it, right?

What do you think God thinks concerning His creations? Do you think that in His mind, He owns *you*? Yes or no?

In my opinion, that's a given, a definite answer of, "Yes, of course, God does!"

Keep in mind that I said *own*, not *control*…

Let's say someone doesn't have a car, but they need one urgently for work. They know that if they can't get to work, they will lose their job, and not having that job will negatively affect their family's welfare. So they go out and steal a car, and claim it as their own. They say to themselves, "I don't have a car, but the car manufacturers have thousands of them, so I'm just going to take one because I need it!"

The car manufacturer made the car and thus has all power and authority over it. But the manufacturer didn't give the car thief permission to take their car; the thief just did it! Now, what do you think will happen once the manufacturer finds out one of their cars is missing? Most certainly, they're going to contact law enforcement and make a report.

Once the police does an investigation and finally tracks down the residence of the one who took the car, they'll likely ask the thief if they happen to know anything about the stolen car. The thief may lie and say no, but the police, on their way in, had already spotted the car parked in the driveway. As the thief attempts to lie and cover up what they did, many intra-conversations will be running wild through their head as they scramble for the right words, in hopes of convincing the police either that they didn't do it, or that the car was theirs!

The thief may be wondering too, *how did the police even figure out that I stole the car? How'd they find me?* No one appeared to be around when they took it…there were no witnesses. *So what brought them straight to my house?* Well, what they didn't realize was that every creator places an "image of ownership" within their creation, which helps them distinguish what belongs to them from what belongs to someone else!

In most new cars today, a tracking device is placed inside. When activated, the tracking device helps the creator, manufacturer, or owner — and the police, too! — locate and connect to that missing creation/property. And the way the owner proves their rightful ownership of the car is a document called a title. The title identifies the creator and owner of the car, in this instance. You cannot own what you did not create, or what you didn't purchase from the creator.

It's also true that every creation knows its creator. God said, *"My sheep hear My voice, and I know them, and they follow Me." (John 10:27)* Inside every creation is something that identifies it as belonging to the one who created it.
Mothers and daughters, allow me to ask you a pointed question:
Are you stealing your body from God??

"How could I steal my body from God?" You may be wondering. The answer is: *when you act as if you "own" it.*
It's not "your" body, to tell you the truth. It's only temporarily given to you. Surprised?

Whenever you are leasing a piece of property, you can be evicted, or the original owner can reclaim whatever it is that they leased to you, at anytime! In other words, you, the lessee, are at the mercy of the owner-creator.
Have you ever heard the term "the body of Christ"? God says in His Word:

"For as the body is one and has many members, but all the members of that one body, being many, are one body, so also is Christ."(1 Corinthians 12:12)

"Now you are the body of Christ, and members individually." (1 Corinthians 12:27)

Just as the auto manufacturer made the car, God made your body. And as stated earlier, He made you for His good pleasure!

God created the body in His image so that it could experience a pleasurable life in the Garden of Eden. And God enjoyed walking and talking in the Garden with this body that was His, which He created. He called that body Adam.

But one day, God came into the Garden, looking for His body, and it was gone! You can imagine that God was probably wondering, "Where is My body?"

He called out loud several times, "Adam! Adam! Adam!" And finally, His body answered, "Yes, Lord?" That's when God noticed that His body wasn't the same body that had walked and talked with Him just the day before. So He began to question His body; He was greatly concerned. "Did you not hear Me when I called you? Where were you? What were you doing? Why were you hiding from me?" And he said, *"I heard thy voice in the garden, and I was afraid, because I was naked; and I hid myself."(Genesis 3:10)*

God knew well the body that He'd created, and this body that stood before Him now was different from the original. God knew this because the body that He'd created knew no shame, while the body in front of Him now was clearly aware of its nakedness and its sins, by eating from the Tree of the Knowledge of Good and Evil, which God had instructed it not to do. As a result, Adam, the body, had gone and hidden-out of shame. But originally, the way God first created it, the body knew no shame, whatsoever!

"And the man and his wife were both naked and were not ashamed." (Genesis 2:25)

God further questioned the body at this point. "Where did you get those ideas from, Adam — who told you that you were naked?"

Adam, The man said, *"The woman whom you gave to be with me, she gave me fruit of the tree, and I ate." (Genesis 3:12)*

"Then the LORD God said to the woman, 'What is this that you have done?' The woman said, 'The serpent deceived me, and I ate.'"

"The LORD God said to the serpent, 'Because you have done this, cursed are you above all livestock and above all beasts of the field; on your belly you shall go, and dust you shall eat all the days of your life.'" (Genesis 3:13-14)

Since this book is about mothers and daughters, let's now go to the first mother, the woman, Eve. As a punishment for the sinful actions she committed along with Adam, God told her:

"I will surely multiply your pain in childbearing; in pain you shall bring forth children.

Your desire shall be for your husband, and he shall rule over you." (Genesis 3:16)

Sound familiar?

Eve was our great-great-great-great-great-great-great ... Grandmother, and we, as mothers and daughters, are still feeling the effects of a wrong decision she made thousands of years ago! The knowledge and revelation of what happened to Mother Eve shed much light on why we mothers and daughters are the way we are, and why we do some of the things we do.

- Why do some of us have a controlling spirit?
- Why do some of us have a lying spirit?
- Why do some of us have a spirit of being ashamed?
- Why do some of us have a spirit of jealousy?
- Why do some of us blame others for decisions we made?
- Why do some of us feel like we don't want to be like our mothers?
- Why do some of us experience such struggle when it comes to the rearing of our daughters?

As God so succinctly put it in Ezekiel 16:44, *"As is the Mother, so is her Daughter."*

It all started with our many-times great-grandmother, Eve, you see. She ended up blaming the serpent, instead of taking responsibility for her actions. That spirit still lives within some mothers and daughters to this day. That's why I tell mothers that there are no perfect daughters, and I tell daughters there are no perfect mothers, and there is no perfect mother-daughter relationship! Yours will always be a relationship in progress. Knowing this, you should do your best to make it the best it can be!

But let's get back to the reason God created the body. God is a spirit. The spirit can't walk, talk touch, smell, or taste the wonderful essences of fruits, vegetables, grass, flowers, animals, fishes, trees, water, air, or other people — none of these things — if it doesn't have a body to dwell in.

God created the body to experience life in the Garden of Eden. The serpent stole this pleasure and authority from the body. Many years later, long after Adam and Eve were evicted from the Garden, God gave His Son, Jesus, a body much like Adam's, and sent Him down to earth to take back man's original authority and fellowship with God. Jesus restored to God's desired pleasurable relationship with the people, mothers and daughters included, of His creation!

Jesus thus reclaimed authority over the body, giving us mothers and daughters the authority to control our individual "bodies of Christ". Now, we can experience the pleasure and freedom of once again having a real, honest relationship with the God, who created us.

Remember, we only have control over our "leased" bodies, for the entirety of our lifespan here on earth, and then we lose it. The body returns to dust, and the spirit returns to God! For the span of time that we're all on earth, God's Word reminds us:

"The thief does not come except to steal, and to kill, and to destroy. I have come that they may have life and that they may have it more abundantly." (John 10:10)

How do you experience life more abundantly, by giving God the opportunity to use your body for Himself, to walk, to talk, and to communicate with the people of His creation in a manner that pleases Him.

And how do you do that? Again, by first accepting Jesus Christ as your Lord and Savior, as you invite Him to come live in your heart. He will come in at your request, and He will share with you a life that you've never before known! He will take you to places of your dreams. He will show you things to come. He will protect you from your enemies. He will bless you with prosperity, and He will grant you good health and a long life! Mothers and Daughters, because God is a gentleman, He will not force His will upon you. He gave you His body, and now it is (temporarily) "yours"; but if you want to experience the fullness of His will for your life, you must allow Him to come and live with you, inside your literal body.

I want you to think about something. Think of all the people who've visited your home in the past. You probably didn't think twice about allowing them to come in, as long as they were pleasant enough at the outset. Some visitors who came through your home, you knew well; others might've come for professional reasons, and you didn't know them at all. Maybe you allowed someone to come over to visit by a recommendation of a family member, a friend, or a consultant, a delivery person, or someone installing a particular service you needed. How did you make the decision so quickly, so confidently, to let them into your home?

God, your Creator, who trust you and have confident in

you gives to you air to breathe. He gave you a body to house your spirit. He gave you a mind to skillfully maintain your health and healing for your body, wealth, and prosperity, wisdom and understanding, unconditional love, grace and mercy, hope, peace, joy, power and authority over the earth, and direct access to Him through Jesus Christ! WOW!

In light of all these amazing blessings and benefits, then, how is it that some people are still trying to decide whether they want to allow God to live inside the bodies He gave them?

Though He clearly owns each one of us (again, because He's the one who created us), because of the ultimate gentleman that He is, God has chosen to give us the final say-so and choice when it comes to a relationship with Him. Still, He cautions us of what is the right choice to make:

"I call heaven and earth as witnesses today against you that I have set before you life and death, blessing and cursing; therefore choose life, that both you and your descendants may live..." (Deuteronomy 30:19)

Mothers and Daughters understand that we are given each day a new chance to change the effects of Eve's sin and punishment on our futures. We can break the generational curse handed down from our many-times great-grandmother, by *choosing life*, as God's Word so clearly instructs us to do!

What do any of us have to lose in making this choice? At least when you're in a relationship with God, you won't have to go desperately searching for Him when you need Him, because He'll already be right there, in an intra-conversation with you! And those of us in fellowship with Him can testify to the fact that He'll walk and talk with you even today, just like He did thousands of years ago with Mother Eve. He'll come and fellowship with you daily — in your own private, "personalized" Garden of Eden!

Chapter Six

God Specially Selects Mothers and Daughters

God not only created you for His good pleasure, He specifically selected your mother to bring you into this world. You already know that you didn't choose your mother, and your mother likewise didn't choose you. But perhaps you didn't know that it was God's personal choice to select your mother for you, and to select you for your mother.

As I said earlier, God sent Jesus to teach us His will and His Word and to demonstrate to us how to properly conduct our lives here on earth, while also prophesying to us of what was to come.

God's Word gives us a strong example of how He selects certain mothers for certain children and vice versa.

The example is that of Mary, the mother of Jesus. God

personally selected her, a virgin, to birth His only Son into the world. It was the Holy Spirit of God that gave Mary conception, following the prophetic word of the angel, Gabriel, who told Mary she would be the mother of the Son of God, the Savior of the entire world. Mary received that word wholeheartedly, with great faith and joy!

Jesus didn't pick Mary to be His mother, and Mary didn't pick Jesus to be her son. God did! He made His perfect will for both of their lives known through His angel:

"And he came to her and said, 'Greetings, O favored one, the Lord is with you!'

"But she was greatly troubled at the saying, and tried to discern what sort of greeting this might be.

"And the angel said to her, 'Do not be afraid, Mary, for you have found favor with God.

"And behold, you will conceive in your womb and bear a son, and you shall call his name Jesus.

"He will be great and will be called the Son of the Most High. And the Lord God will give to him the throne of his father David, and he will reign over the house of Jacob forever, and of his kingdom there will be no end.'

"And Mary said to the angel, 'How will this be, since I am a virgin?'

"And the angel answered her, 'The Holy Spirit will come upon you, and the power of the Most High will overshadow you; therefore the child to be born will be called holy—the Son of

God.'

"And behold, your relative Elizabeth in her old age has also conceived a son, and this is the sixth month with her who was called barren.

"For nothing will be impossible with God."

"And Mary said, 'Behold, I am the servant of the Lord; let it be to me according to your word.' And the angel departed from her.

"In those days Mary arose and went with haste into the hill country, to a town in Judah, and she entered the house of Zechariah and greeted Elizabeth.

"And when Elizabeth heard the greeting of Mary, the baby leaped in her womb. And Elizabeth was filled with the Holy Spirit, and she exclaimed with a loud cry, 'Blessed are you among women, and blessed is the fruit of your womb!

"And why is this granted to me that the mother of my Lord should come to me For behold, when the sound of your greeting came to my ears, the baby in my womb leaped for joy.

"And blessed is she who believed that there would be a fulfillment of what was spoken to her from the Lord.'

"And Mary said, 'My soul magnifies the Lord, and my spirit rejoices in God my Savior, for he has looked on the humble estate of his servant. For behold, from now on all generations will call me blessed; for he who is mighty has done great things for me, and holy is his name. And his mercy is for those who fear him from generation to generation.'" (Luke 1:28-50)

So, Mothers, be encouraged to know that God has personally hand-picked you to be the mother of _____. *(Please write your daughter's name here.)*

Mary is a godly example of how you, Mother, were selected to become the mother of a specific child.

Who knows — maybe like Mary, you also received a word from a heavenly messenger about the birth of your child! But even if you didn't, the Holy Spirit inside you confirmed that you were pregnant, possibly even the very moment you conceived. Whether you wanted to believe it or not, you somehow knew, didn't you? Think about it!

I remember the moment I conceived my daughter. I felt something leap in my womb. I immediately said to my husband, "I'm pregnant!"

"How do you know?" he asked.

"I just felt something jump inside my womb! I just know I'm pregnant."

And I did know — beyond a shadow of a doubt! That was in September, on a Labor Day weekend. My daughter, who is our only child, was born the following June.

Immediately after I conceived, my spirit started telling me things I needed to stop eating and stop doing, as well as what I needed to start doing, to deliver a healthy baby. We mothers get the warnings, for sure, whether from inside ourselves, or from other mothers, or from our doctors.

Ultimately, it is up to us to decide whether our actions

will be by the laws of health, as well as God's Word. As any pediatrician will tell you, your choices make all the difference in the wellness of your unborn daughter, even to the point of influencing the growing baby's temperament.

Here is where I think that I should share some of the imitate details of my own pregnancy!

But, before I get into those details, I want to share my thoughts when I was a young girl about having a baby. I remembered one of the ladies in my neighborhood that seemed to have a baby every year! As soon as she had one baby, a few months, she would be pregnant again!

One of her pregnancies made a major impact on my life. In middle school, I got off the school bus and as I was walking home I saw the lady's small children outside the window watching and listening to the screaming voice of their mother having their baby sister! Of course, I joined them and watched as well. As we peeped into the window, trying not to be seen, I immediately realized that my mother, as well as several other ladies from the neighborhood, was in the room helping the midwife deliver the baby! I remember thinking to myself, how in the world that BIG baby could come out of her! It was at that moment I decided that I was never going to have a baby. I couldn't imagine a baby coming out of me! No, No, not me!

As we stood outside of the window, one of the younger children began to cry. As I started to comfort him we all suddenly heard the call for the last hard push and then there was a spanking and then the piercing cry of a newborn baby. We started dancing around and laughing. Then they announced that she had a girl! They cleaned her up and they called her brothers and sisters, and me, to come inside to see the new baby. We were so excited!

Then it came time to name the baby. They kept asking the mother what she was going to name her. Well, she had six children already. As she was thinking of a name I yelled out, "Can I name her?" The mother looked at me and said, yes, and without thinking a name came out of my mouth! I told her I wanted to name her Angela Deanna! Her mother said that's a pretty name. We will name her Angela Deanna. At that moment, in my mind, she became my baby. I took a personal interest in her. I would come home from school, change my clothes, eat, and rush over to see 'my baby'. I would sit and hold her for hours. I couldn't believe that her mother allowed me to name her; after all, I was just a child. I would buy her things and I called her my baby! About a year and a half after she was born the family moved to New Jersey and it broke my heart. I haven't seen her since!

As time passed, I still had no desire to ever physical have a baby! I kept those painful images and sounds of childbirth in my head for years. Every time they came forth I would mentally say, "Oh no, not me!"

Another thought that I had in my mind from my childhood was that I was never getting married. Well, I got married at the age of 18, two months after high school! After being married for three-and-a-half years and not getting pregnant, a thought came to my mind, saying that I better be careful because my luck was running out! From that thought, I decided that maybe I should start taking some type of birth control. I felt in my spirit that I was headed toward getting pregnant! So, I went to my doctor and got a prescription for birth control pills. Once I started taking them I thought that I didn't have to worry about getting pregnant! After taking the pills for about two weeks, I started having migraine headaches! I went back to my doctor and I told him that my head felt like it was going to pop wide open! He did his usual checkup and discovered that it was coming from the effects of the birth control pills. I made an immediate decision right then that I was no longer going to take birth control pills! Of course, the doctor tried to get me to try a different type of birth control pill with less strength. I told him that I was done with birth control. The doctor then tried to tell me that my body has been exposed to a medicine and that may increase my chances of getting pregnant! I thanked him. As I left the doctor's office that day I had no fear of this happening because it just wouldn't happen to me. I am not going to get pregnant!

Two weeks later, Labor Day weekend…I got pregnant! During the time of my pregnancy, I constantly kept praying. I would ask God questions like:
- How will I know what to do?
- How will I know how to take care of a baby, I am an only twenty-one and a half?
- How can a "BABY" come out of me?

Like most young pregnant women, I immediately got the books and started reading. Like many mothers, my mother never talked to me about having a baby. She was so busy talking to me about how not to have a baby! Remember, I got married two months after high school.

I didn't know how to tell my mother that I was pregnant. In my mind, that would confirm that I was having sex! Although we were very close, I couldn't figure out how to tell her, and I was married!

I had a very smooth pregnancy. However, when it came to food I was my worst enemy! I had a thought in my mind that I was eating for two people, so I gave myself the authority to eat as much as I wanted! Well, 9-months later I was 52 pounds heavier. I looked like I was pregnant with twins. My doctor had warned me that if I had gained one pound, by my next visit, he was going to send me straight to the hospital. I didn't believe him, so I didn't take him seriously. Two weeks after that warning I gained seven pounds. I then cut back on my food intake, but on my next visit the doctor told my husband to take me straight to the hospital. I got upset and asked, what's wrong? He looked at me and said, "Seven pounds!" I was shocked, and all I could think about was the food that I had cooked before I went to the doctor's office: Collard greens, rice, bake chicken, cornbread, and an apple pie. All homemade!

I tried to sweet talk my husband to take me home to get my bag. I told him at least we could have dinner together before we went to the hospital. That didn't work.

I spent five days in the hospital. The first three days spent was getting rid of the water weight that I was carrying that was preventing me from going into labor.

Now, the shocker was that I could only have Jell-O and ginger ale! I was mad! My mother-in-law, whom I love dearly worked at the hospital. One of the nurses told her that I was upset because I couldn't have something to eat. My mother-in-law came to my room and reminded me of the many conversations that she and my mother had with me concerning my food intake and about gaining so much weight. As I laid in the bed crying from hunger, I turned and looked at my mother's face, filled with grief. She couldn't bear to see me want for anything and surely not for food! My mother-in-law left the room and came back with two single packs of salt-less crackers and told me to eat them and get it together!

The doctor later came into the room and said that he had to burst my water bag to begin labor. When I saw that long piece of metal in his hand I told him that there is no way he was going to stick that in me. So he went back and got one that was made out of plastic. I was so afraid; I started crying! How was I ever going to have a "Big" baby.

After he burst my water bag, about 15-20 minutes later, my mother saw an expression on my face and knew that we were having a baby! However, just before they came to move me to the delivery room, I was told that my doctor took sick and that I would have another doctor! What! All I kept thinking was whether this doctor knew what he was doing!

For the next few hours, I experienced pain that I didn't think was humanly possible!

I kept reminding the doctor that I was supposed to be put to sleep and he kept reminding me that I had to wait. I can remember one of the nurses asking me if this was my first pregnancy. I told her it was my first, and my last! As I brutally flapped my hospital gown to help me manage the pain, I kept praying. I said, "Lord if you help me to get through this, I promise you that I will never be in this position again!"
My daughter was born eight hours later.

As I work with mothers and daughters today, I am constantly reminded of when the nurse placed my daughter in my arms. The feelings that I felt when I first looked into her eyes, and when I counted her fingers and toes, removed all memory of the pain! I forgot all about the pain that I endured when I felt her heart beat in rhythm with mine.

My husband, mother, father, and mother-in-law and I prayed over her and gave thanks to God. She was a beautiful 8 pounds and 7 ounces baby girl made of Pure Love! I knew at that moment that my life had changed forever.

I asked God another question, "Would you please help me with our daughter and teach me what I need to know, and show me the things I need to be aware of concerning her life?" That was a few years ago! During those times you had to wait to find out if you were having a girl or a boy. However, my mother told me from the first few months of my pregnancy that I was having a girl. When I got pregnant I asked God for a girl. I was thinking more of treating her like a doll baby.

I had no idea that God had already selected my daughter and He couldn't have picked a better daughter for me!

God also knew that He had appointed me, before the beginning of time, to minister to mothers and their daughters. He knew that I had to experience raising a daughter in order to know how mothers and daughters interact. I had my experiences with my mother, she and I were very close and loved each other so much; I really miss my mother. My mother, Pearl, has made her transition back home. I thank God for choosing her to be my mother. She was the "Best" mother for me! She gave me the best gift ever, she gave me Jesus! She would say to me from the time I was very small: "I want you to know when you can't get to me or your daddy, just call on Jesus!" At the age of five, I remember having conversations with God. Thank you, mother!

Earlier, I told you that I was given the opportunity to name my neighbor's baby? I named her Angela Deanna. For years I couldn't figure out where that name came from. Even my mother asked me how I came up with that name. I didn't know; it just popped out of my mouth! After giving birth to my baby the nurses kept coming into my room for three days asking for a name for my baby. I had chosen so many names I couldn't narrow them down to one. On the fourth day, the nurse came back to my room. She wasn't leaving until I gave her a name. All of a sudden I said Angela Deanna!

Isn't that amazing?

I've been praying and seeking God for instructions and guidance concerning her life and our relationship for more than 40 years and God has helped us through it all! Now, we pray for each other, and for any situation that comes up in our lives and the lives of our family.

Mothers, God is depending on us to depend on Him!

This is why God holds you accountable for the outcome of your daughter. He gave you special instruction from the moment you conceived your daughter. In fact, God is your instruction source for nurturing your daughter from start to finish — He's the One who created our daughters, after all, so He's the Source of all knowledge concerning them! You can download your instructions from Him on a daily basis, too. All you have to do is ask.

And for those of you who are mothers of teenage and adult daughters, if you feel that it's too late for you to turn things around and make a difference in her life because you've already made so many mistakes, just know that it is in fact NOT too late!

Again, this book will remind you of your ability to repent for all your mistakes and start all over again. All what's required is that you stop whatever it is you're doing incorrectly, adopt new ways of coping, behaving, and dealing with your daughter, and ask God for continual guidance. He *will* help you!

Again, *"Ask, and it will be given to you; seek, and you will find; knock, and it will be opened to you". (Matthew 7:7)* Remember, God is waiting on YOU!

Chapter Seven

Wisdom for Mothers and Daughters

Wisdom for Mothers

When you ask God for help, you get God's wisdom. His Word says:

"If any of you lacks wisdom, let him ask of God, who gives to all liberally and without reproach, and it will be given to him." (James 1:5)

God has provided many scriptures in the Bible that contain His infinite wisdom, many of which are specifically directed to us, Mothers, to increase our wisdom as parents. Some of these nuggets of truth and sound instruction may be considered as "pearls of wisdom."

"Pearls of wisdom" are special words that you take in and add to your knowledge as a mother, and you should also drop some of them into the conscious mind of your daughter.

This way, as the word leaves her conscious mind, they will find their way into her subconscious mind, where they will remain forever! Those words will subsequently create an image in her mind that will affect her decision-making abilities for the rest of her life. Her self-esteem, too, is a creation of your pearls of wisdom or lack thereof!

A mother's wisdom should come from a place of love, acceptance, forgiveness, peace, joy, hope, trust, and honesty. The tone in which you deliver your words also matters greatly, Mothers, because of the way you say something creates in your daughter's mind her understanding of the meaning behind your words.

It is, therefore, a good idea to occasionally ask your daughter to repeat back to you what you've said to her, just to make sure she's correctly interpreting and clearly understanding your meaning. That is the only way you'll know whether you are communicating with her effectively.

Pearls of wisdom, by the way, are always Good News!

Here are a few more precious "pearls" from our Heavenly Father:

"The fear of the LORD is the beginning of wisdom; all those who practice it have a good understanding. His praise endures forever!" (Psalms 111:10)

"Can a woman forget her nursing child, that she should have no compassion on the son of her womb? Even these may forget, yet I will not forget you." (Isaiah 49:15)

"Train up a child in the way he should go, and when he is old he will not depart from it." (Proverbs 22:6)

"The rod and rebuke give wisdom, but a child left to himself brings shame to his mother."(Proverbs 29:15)

"How much better to get wisdom than gold! And to get understanding is to be chosen rather than silver." (Proverbs 16: 16)

"And these words which I command you today shall be in your heart. You shall teach them diligently to your children, and shall talk of them when you sit in your house, when you walk by the way, when you lie down, and when you rise up." (Deuteronomy 6:6-7)

Wisdom for Daughters

Okay, Mothers, so you know what this means, right? It means your daughter is going to require your help in reading and properly interpreting the Word of God. And if you haven't introduced her to the Bible yet, understand that there is no blame here, but you need to go ahead and do so. Simply start where you are, and start right now!

Daughters, listen to your mothers and search the Word of God for yourself as well. If you're reading this book, I'm assuming that you're of a certain age, which means you're mature enough to start reading and understanding the Bible for yourself!

God's best advice to His daughters is for them to give honor to their parents.

Daughters, you get big rewards from God when you honor your mother. You get good health, as well as longer, blessed days here on earth!

God offers more of His infinite wisdom in the following passages:

"Honor your father and mother, which is the first commandment with promise…" (Ephesians 6:2)

You know the commandments: Do not murder, Do not commit adultery, Do not steal, Do not bear false witness, Do not defraud, Honor your father and mother. (Mark 10:19)

And he said, *"May you be blessed by the Lord, my daughter. You have made this last kindness greater than the first in that you have not gone after young men, whether poor or rich. And now, my daughter, do not fear. I will do for you all that you ask, for all my fellow townsmen know that you are a worthy woman." (Ruth 3:10-11)*

"Behold, every one that useth proverbs shall use this proverb against thee, saying, As is the Mother, so is her Daughter." (Ezekiel 16:44)

Wisdom for Motherless Daughters

God's wisdom and advice are for all of His daughters. Daughters, some of you may no longer have the presence of an earthly mother, and it may be that your father is absent from your life, as well. But understand that you will always have a Heavenly Father, who is your very Creator, God Himself!

Just as God blessed Esther, an orphan, to marry a worldly king and save her people from slaughter, God can use you! So when you start feeling like you're all alone, and nobody loves or is there for you, just read the book of Esther. You will see in this book the power, planning, and compassion of God, and you'll be inspired, as well, by the queenly qualities of Esther. After all, those same qualities live in you!

God wants to share with you, just as He did with Esther, He can put you in the right place at the right time, in a way that will turn your life completely around!

God placed Esther in the right home, to be reared by just the right person, at the right time!

"And He brought up Hadassah, that is, Esther, his uncle's daughter: for she had neither father nor mother, And maid was fair and beautiful; whom Mordecai, when her father and mother were dead, took for his own daughter." (Esther 2:7)

Now, think about the people that God has sent into your life to help you. Through them, God is demonstrating that He is always with you and that He will never leave you. He purposefully touches the hearts of certain men and women in your path, to have them help meet your needs here on earth! Just as God used Esther, He will use you, too — if you allow Him to!

Wisdom for Grandmothers

Grandmother, you've no doubt lived many of your years raising your daughter with trials and errors, as they say. You've raised your daughter up, and figured your job was done, only to discover, perhaps, that it's not over!

Raising a daughter from conception to age eighteen surely defines her as a legal adult, but it doesn't mean she's truly all grown up. She's just starting to experience things in the "real world," outside the safety and protection of your home, making this a period in her life where she's going to need your advice. It seems like it should be the opposite, right? Like she should finally be independent, and able to put into action all the wisdom and training you gave her over the years?

"So you are saying that my job's still not done, that I have to continue parenting an adult?" you're probably asking. Yes, and I can tell you that it won't be easy. The tone of your conversations will have to be different with your adult daughter, for starters, so when she questions you about something, you'll no longer be able to get away with, "Because I said so!"

No, that tactic won't work on your adult daughter. She'll be coming to you for real answers now, concerning serious life and parenting issues. And it may be the case that your grandmotherly involvement and input are required, as well, as she goes about rearing her daughter!

So, now you're a grandmother, you're probably

wondering to yourself, "How in the world do I handle this? Am I responsible for my adult daughter and her daughter?"

Well, the Good News is that there's no need to worry about how you'll handle your daughter's "adult level" questions and issues. When she comes to you saying, "Hey, Mom, I need your advice," just remember that God created and handpicked you for your daughter, and He specially selected her for you. He, therefore, holds the answer to any and all questions either of you will ever have, offering solutions and provisions to your every need. His Word says:

"If any of you lacks wisdom, let him ask of God, who gives to all liberally and without reproach, and it will be given to him." (James 1:5)

Specifically, to grandmothers, God also says:

"Older women likewise are to be reverent in behavior, not slanderers or slaves to much wine. They are to teach what is good, and so train the young women to love their husbands and children, to be self-controlled, pure, working at home, kind, and submissive to their own husbands, that the word of God may not be reviled." (Titus 2:3-5)

Wisdom for Mothers-In-Law and Daughters-In-Law

Mother-in-law, realize that you ought to love your daughter-in-law just as you would your biological daughter. When you gain a daughter-in-law, you should simply consider her your "next daughter in line" — your last, or "youngest" daughter, following the one you birthed! In other words, if you're the mother of three daughters and a son, and your son marries, his new wife just became your fourth daughter!

At the same time, Mother, you've just gained a daughter-in-law, one that you're now considering like your daughter. Do both of yourselves a favor and DON'T try to raise her again!

After all, she already has (or had) a biological mother and the two of them have/had their relationship. Allow your daughter-in-law, then, to first and foremost be the wife of your son; you owe her that, whether the two of them are living in your house, as some new couples do, or not. Show her respect as a wife and love her as a daughter, and expect her to love and respect you in return. It starts with you. Just — again — keep in mind that she's raised!

(Remember, too, that a loving relationship with your daughter-in-law leads to a loving relationship with — and full access to — any future granddaughters from that union!)

Daughter-in-law, for your part, be mindful to treat your mother-in-law with the same respect you're expected to show your mother. Notice I said expected to, because the reality is that not all daughters properly respect their mothers. And if they don't, they usually don't know how to show respect to their mother-in-law, either.

The Good News, nevertheless, at any time, if you don't know what to do or say in a given situation regarding your mother-in-law or daughter-in-law, God has the answer! His Word advises:

"If any of you lacks wisdom, let him ask of God, who gives to all liberally and without reproach, and it will be given to him." (James 1:5)

God gives us an ideal example of an incredibly loving and respectful mother-in-law/daughter-in-law relationship in the story of Ruth.

In the following passage, Ruth verbally expresses a powerful love for her mother-in-law, Naomi. Ruth was one truly God-fearing daughter-in-law! She refused to leave the side of Naomi, even after her husband and Naomi's son had died. Naomi, after all, was the one who had taught Ruth about the one true God; it wasn't her birth mother who'd taught her, but her mother-in-law!

But Ruth said, *"Do not urge me to leave you or to return from following you. For where you go I will go and where you lodge I will lodge. Your people shall be my people and your God my God. Where you die I will die, and there will I be buried. May the Lord do so to me and more also if anything but death parts me from you." (Ruth 1:16-17)*

Ruth was willing to lay down her life for her mother-in-law, which speaks volumes about Naomi's character and values.

So, I have a question for you, Reader. If you happen to be married, or the mother of a married son, what is the nature of your relationship with your mother-in-law, or daughter-in-law?

If it's not what it should be — if it doesn't line up with the beautiful example set by Ruth and Naomi — here's a tip: Love and compassion are the key ingredients to forming a loving, trusting, bonding relationship with your respective in-law. Just read Ruth!

Wisdom for Barren Women

God, in His infinite love for mothers and daughters, has made ample provision for all of them.

When you hear the word "barren," you probably instantly think "infertile, unproductive, sterile, or unfruitful," the literal definition. Because of the strong desire, many women have to bear children, as well as the stigma commonly associated with those who can't, many barren women figure that God has forgotten them. Their question to Him is, "What's wrong with me — why didn't you bless me to have a child?"

These women may sometimes even feel that they've done something wrong in their past and that it's somehow their fault. Otherwise, why would a loving God withhold from them the blessing of motherhood?

If you are barren, know that God is speaking to you right now. He wants you to know that He has chosen you to be the mother of many children, though perhaps not biologically. Your love for children is so deep, concentrated, innocent, and pure, that you're able to "spiritually connect" to children without ever having had one attached to your physical body!

You have the capacity to connect mentally and spiritually with children. God wants to use you to be the Sarah in the children's lives, in other words. What an honor!

Sarah was considered to be an incredibly beautiful, patient, loving woman. Initially, Sarah was barren. And although she at first questioned God concerning His promise to her and her husband that they would have a son, and she even laughed out loud about it, Sarah nevertheless was a special woman of God — chosen, as Abraham's counterpart, to be the "mother of many nations"!

At the ripe old age of ninety, in fact, when her husband was himself a hundred years old, Sarah finally conceived and gave birth to her very first child, a son named Isaac. Through Isaac's birth, she experienced the fulfillment of God's precious promise of motherhood to her. What a miracle! Be encouraged by her testimony.

"And I will bless her and also give you a son by her; then I will bless her, and she shall be a mother of nations; kings of peoples shall be from her.

"Then Abraham fell on his face and laughed, and said in his heart, 'Shall a child be born to a man who is one hundred years old? And shall Sarah, who is ninety years old, bear a child?' And Abraham said to God, 'Oh, that Ishmael might live before You!'

"Then God said: 'No, Sarah your wife shall bear you

a son, and you shall call his name Isaac; I will establish My covenant with him for an everlasting covenant, and with his descendants after him.' " (Genesis 17:16-19)

So, even though Sarah struggled a bit in her faith, God still honored her by keeping His Word to her and making her the mother of the nation of Israel. She lived to be one hundred and twenty-seven years old, giving her more than enough years to rear her son lovingly and see him to adulthood.

According to statistics, the majority of women give birth to between one and seven children. But as a barren mother, you have an unlimited number of children. God can use you to mother them, in their special times of need!

I believe that a mother is selected to parent a certain personality-type in a child. But a barren mother, on the other hand, has been selected to mother many different types of personalities, because God knew she could handle it — that she was up to the task!

As I write this special message to you from God Himself, know that this is a unique perspective that He's given me, for the barren woman. God wants you to consider the fact that He must truly love you, given that He trusts you with so many of His children! Again, what an honor!

He has this to say concerning you too:

"He gives the barren woman a home, making her the joyous mother of children. Praise the LORD!" (Psalm 113:9)

God's Advice for Daughters

Daughters, God have used me to share some of His wisdom with you throughout this book, but He wants to expand your knowledge with this added advice:

"Do not rebuke an older man but encourage him as you would a father, younger men as brothers, older women as mothers, younger women as sisters, in all purity. "(I Timothy 5:1-2)

"But the Helper, the Holy Spirit, whom the Father will send in my name, he will teach you all things and bring to your remembrance all that I have said to you." (John 14:26)

Daughters, those are words directly from God to you. I would, therefore, advise you to listen to them very closely, and also follow them!

A Daughter's Thanks to God

Daughters, because of the love, wisdom, and advice to you from God, you ought to just take a moment and sincerely thank Him! Consider this powerful scripture about how awesomely He made you, after all:

"For you formed my inward parts; you knitted me together in my mother's womb. I praise you, for I am fearfully and wonderfully made. Wonderful are your works; my soul knows it very well. My frame was not hidden from you when I

was being made in secret, intricately woven in the depths of the earth. Your eyes saw my unformed substance; in your book were written, every one of them, the days that were formed for me, when as yet there was none of them." (Psalm139:13-16)

With a genuinely grateful heart, tell the Lord:
"I am grateful, Lord, and I thank You for loving me and creating me for your good pleasure!"

Chapter Eight

The Standard of the Virtuous Woman

For Both Mothers And Daughters
The 'Proverbs 31' Woman: A Woman Who Fears God

Who can find a virtuous woman? for her price is far above rubies.
The heart of her husband doth safely trust in her, so that he shall have no need of spoil.
She will do him good and not evil all the days of her life.
She seeketh wool, and flax, and worketh willingly with her hands.
She is like the merchants' ships; she bringeth her food from afar.
She riseth also while it is yet night, and giveth meat to her household, and a portion to her maidens.

She considereth a field, and buyeth it: with the fruit of her hands she planteth a vineyard.
She girdeth her loins with strength, and strengtheneth her arms.
She perceiveth that her merchandise is good: her candle goeth not out by night.
She layeth her hands to the spindle, and her hands hold the distaff.
She stretcheth out her hand to the poor; yea, she reacheth forth her hands to the needy.
She is not afraid of the snow for her household: for all her household are clothed with scarlet.
She maketh herself coverings of tapestry; her clothing is silk and purple.
Her husband is known in the gates, when he sitteth among the elders of the land.
She maketh fine linen, and selleth it; and delivereth girdles unto the merchant.
Strength and honour are her clothing; and she shall rejoice in time to come.
She openeth her mouth with wisdom; and in her tongue is the law of kindness.
She looketh well to the ways of her household, and eateth not the bread of idleness.
Her children arise up, and call her blessed; her husband also, and he praiseth her.

The Standard of the Virtuous Woman

Many daughters have done virtuously, but thou excellest them all.
Favour is deceitful, and beauty is vain: but a woman that feareth the LORD, she shall be praised.
Give her of the fruit of her hands; and let her own works praise her in the gates.

Chapter Nine

Congratulations Mother...it's a Girl!

Think about this fact, Mothers: God gives the gift of life to you, as He brings life through you.

As stated earlier, God handpicked you to be the mother for your particular daughter. A piece of God's actual Spirit is placed into your unborn daughter; then it was birthed through you when you brought her into the world. That spirit of life was actually inside her before she drew her very first breath, long before the doctor spanked her behind! You may recall that moment pretty vividly when your daughter took her first gulps of natural air! The air entered her lungs, and she breathed it back out with a sharp cry, signaling the start of her new life here on earth!

It was at that moment that you became a new mother (or a "mother anew," if you'd already given birth before), and that precious little one became your unique, unlike-any-other daughter!

After her birth, the doctor wrapped her in a blanket and placed her in your arms; then, the bonding process began. The first thing a new mother often does when she first takes her infant into her arms (after giving thanks to God) is lovingly take in her daughter's face, body, and limbs; then she counts her fingers and toes. Mom's just trying to make sure God didn't miss anything! As I explained, the tiny being that you delivered to the world at that point came with the Spirit of God inside of her. The Spirit of God serves as the overseer of the body, as the body houses the spirit. The body will one day die, but the spirit will live on eternally.

That spirit came with an intended purpose. It came here so that God could share the richness of His presence with it, and so that it would, in turn, glorify Him. Understand, Mother, that as the Spirit of God lay quietly within your baby's body, that spirit hears and understands what you say and do to it. The Spirit of God also knows your intentions toward the baby and the proper way to treat it. The Spirit of God is both inside the baby's body and hovering outside it, carefully watching. In other words, be careful what you do. God is watching you!

Some mothers may think that because they birthed a baby, it belongs to them. It does, in one sense but then, in another sense, it doesn't. Why? Because we simply can't "own" what belongs to God. Remember that I said earlier — you can't own what you didn't create, or what you haven't purchased!

The baby is a body and spirit belonging to God, which enters into the world to create its own, personalized "Garden of Eden" within the overall Garden that is the earth. Because the world has become so divided by so many different beliefs and religions, it's an incredible challenge to get all of us back to God's original intent and purpose when He created the Garden of Eden. His Word declares of His people,

"They are not of the world, even as I am not of the world." (John 17:16)

As I see it, this means that while our bodies are here on earth, our minds, souls, and spirits are located in heaven. At the same time, we have been given the power and the authority to take dominion over the entire natural world.

How do we accomplish this? How do we take dominion over the world?

We achieve dominion by creating our very own, personalized Garden of Eden here on earth. If you look around, you can see evidence of different "personalized gardens" that have already been created and taken shape. They are called "rich and successful" people.

Who are the world's rich and successful? They're individuals who've tapped into a belief system that works, according to the Word of God. His Word frequently says "whosoever" and "whatsoever," and these people have believed and received! (Mark 11:23)

Remember, we came to this earth in a body and given

the gift of life inside of a mind, soul, and spirit. So what is it that differentiates one body's experience from that of another body? It's who those two bodies happen to believe in, as well as what they believe; that makes all the difference!

Mothers, as I've said before, God is holding you personally responsible for the outcome of your daughters, who are His daughters…He has simply entrusted you with them. He is expecting you to serve as a virtuous example for your daughter, impressing upon her mind and spirit a godly image that she will one day become herself. Again, that's why His Word says,
"As is the Mother, so is her Daughter." (Ezekiel 16:44)

Ponder these questions: What type of role model are you for your daughter? What images and impressions are you making on her mind today to influence who she becomes in the future?

A Few Thoughts On Life Itself

"And the LORD God formed man of the dust of the ground, and breathed into his nostrils the breath of life, and man became a living being." (Genesis 2:7)

As strange as it may sound, life is between breaths! I was so intrigued by this thought that I decided to count my breaths one day, and I discovered that I average about thirteen to fourteen inhale/exhales per minute. If we use thirteen breaths per minute as an average, then, we get an approximate 18,720 breaths that most of us take on a daily basis!

What's important to realize here is that each breath that you take represents God's breathing into your nostrils new life on a moment-by-moment basis. With each exhale you take a temporary loss of life, while the next inhale represents a renewal of life.

Obviously, as long as you continue to inhale, you're still alive, but there will come a day when you make your final exhale. At that point when you take your very last exhale, your body will die.

Here's a pointed question to challenge you: **"What will you be noted for accomplishing between your first breath and your very last exhale?"**

My advice to you is that with every breath give thanks unto God — recognizing that He is the giver of your life and the very air that you breathe, with the power and purpose to sustain you for as long as your mission remains incomplete on this earth!

Now *that's* some *Good News!*

Food for Mothers and Daughters

We obviously have a variety of options when it comes to the foods we consume for our bodies. There are the foods that we like, the foods we don't like at all, and the foods we eat mainly because our bodies require them to stay healthy.

As women, mothers and daughters are particularly conscious of their bodies, constantly checking them on a daily basis. We regularly change, alter, remake, reshape, and redefine our bodies, our hair, our makeup, and our wardrobe, in a constant effort to make ourselves pleasing and acceptable.

Many of us also watch television, listen to the radio, read magazines and observe other women's habits and tastes to obtain cues for recreating ourselves. Sadly, most of these things are done to impress other people, which really shouldn't be our goal.

Most women think that if they look stylish and up-to-date on the outside, people will think they are stylish and up-to-date on the inside, too. Well, as a Christian clinical psychologist, I can't tell you the number of mothers and daughters who've come into my office looking like they just stepped out of a magazine, but their souls and spirits look like they've been homeless and wandering the streets for years!

Whenever I see this it's obvious to me that the minds of many of these women are totally confused and tied up in endless intra-conversations. In other words they're "unequally yoked," with their stunning outer appearances!

Being an ordained chaplain, as well, during my assessments of clients, one of my first questions is typically this: "Are you saved?"

"Yes!" a few of them will reply. Others tell me a direct "No." The answer I get from the majority of them, is more like,

"Well..."

If hesitance and uncertainty are the answer I get, I make a point to choose my words wisely from there. If they've told me anything other than an emphatic "Yes!" I respectfully ask them, "Would you like to receive the blessings and benefits that God has for you?"

I then assure them that God has provided an answer and solution to any situation that may arise in their life, answers that can all be found in the Bible and through prayer!

I also let them know that they don't have to live in a confused, fearful state of mind because God promised them a sound mind:

"For God hath not given us the spirit of fear, but of power, and of love, and of a sound mind." (II Timothy 1:7)

To obtain that "soundness" of mind, all you have to do is receive it. It's one of God's promises, to you!

Whenever a client indicates to me that they may have accepted Christ in the past, but they're unsure about the present condition of their soul, I tell them this: "Just to make sure that you are Saved, let's take a moment to pray the prayer of salvation before going any further."

If they agree, once they've prayed the prayer of salvation, I consider them now ready for Christian counseling! Their mind is now prepared to receive the Word of God, as well as His advice for their lives as expressed to me — based on my spiritual knowledge and professional experience. That is what I consider being the proper order for receiving Christian counseling!

A Mother and Daughter's Best Life Now

The promises of God are His personal guarantees that what He says is what you'll get if you obey and believe Him! We've already established that God is not a man that he should lie.

"God is not a man, that he should lie; neither the son of man, that he should repent: hath he said, and shall he not do it? or hath he spoken, and shall he not make it good?" (Numbers 23:19)

If He's not a man who lies, it simply means that all the words contained within His promises must be true and fail-proof!

If you believe this, then you should wholeheartedly agree with this thought: **I can completely rely on God's word, resting assured that it will <u>always</u> come to pass!**

When God sent Moses to deliver the Ten Commandments to His people, the children of Israel. I believe He did so because He wanted His people to get an understanding of His love and expectations for them. But, when the people only grew worse in sin, I believe God stood back and made a decision right then and there, which showed up many years later. He decided to create a human experience for His only Son, Jesus, who would serve as an example to His wayward, disobedient people. He came to show us that man can live according to the will and Word of God!

I believe it was then that God determined He would create a fleshly body, let it be in the womb of a virgin mother (Mary) through the Holy Ghost, and let that child be born a Savior to the entire world. It's a bit of a mystery, but Jesus was God Himself, being born through a woman. God made it known ahead of time that this new, human version of Himself would be called Jesus! Because His chosen people weren't appearing to understand who He was as God, and they clearly weren't recognizing either the magnitude of the power He'd placed inside of them; God decided to send Jesus. He permitted Jesus to come to earth as a man to bring back into focus His original will and plan, while also granting each human being direct access to Him.

God then came to the natural world as "Jesus" to demonstrate to us how to best communicate and fellowship with Him, and how to use God's very words to activate the manifestations of whatever we need at any given time.

God desires a personal relationship with each of us. He wants to show you, mothers and daughters, how to enjoy the lifestyle He designed specifically for you, and he expects you, Mother, to teach these same words, concepts, and principles to your daughter, just as He taught them to his own dear Son, Jesus. Likewise, Daughter, God expects you to be as receptive and obedient to His Word, as expressed through your mother, as Jesus was to God!

Jesus' life is the example that we should follow, and His power to completely obey God and effect miracles came from His adherence to the words of God! That is why Jesus made it known,

"For I have not spoken of myself; but the Father, which sent me, he gave me a commandment, what I should say, and what I should speak." (John 12:49)

"For the Father loveth the Son, and sheweth him all things that himself doeth: and he will shew him greater works than these, that ye may marvel." (John 5:20)

"Then said Jesus unto them, 'When ye have lifted up the Son of man, then shall ye know that I am he and that I do nothing of myself; but as my Father hath taught me, I speak these things.'"
(John 8:28)

In other words, Jesus neither said nor did anything He didn't receive instructions from God to say or do!

Now, if Jesus had to use the words of God to perform miracles, whose words do you think you should be using to perform miracles in your life?

If you want the same results that Jesus got, you would be wise to use the same words that Jesus was successful in using! God is reliable and faithful to His promises, and His Word is the power that activates those promises. To see His promises manifested in your life, you must:

- First, identify the particular promise of God you desire to see manifested in your life.
- Next, speak the words of Scripture out loud, asking your Father God to activate His Words in your life, in the name of Jesus!
- Next, have faith in God that He will do what He's promised — what His Word says He will do.
- Finally, allow Him time to bring forth the manifestation of that particular promise in your life!

It's in the timing, by the way, or the passage of time, that's the period when many mothers and daughters lose their faith. The time between when they asked and when they finally receive may seem long, but it's a necessary part of the process, so don't give up! You may be just a few moments away, from the manifestation of the blessings that you've been faithfully, believing God!

The Good News is that you placed your "order" or prayer with God, in the name of Jesus, the fulfillment of that order is guaranteed. So, please, whatever you do, wait patiently for the delivery of it!

Chapter Ten

A Mother and Daughter's Ultimate Weapon

Mothers and daughters, when you think of a weapon, what's the first thought that comes to your mind? I guess most of you will immediately get an image of a gun. Am I right?

We know that almost any object can be used as a weapon, depending on whose hands it's in, a "weapon" is defined as: Any device used with intent to inflict damage or harm to living beings, structures, or systems. Weapons are used to increase the efficacy and efficiency of activities such as crime, law enforcement, self-defense, and warfare. In a broader context, weapons may be construed to include anything used to gain a strategic, material or mental advantage over an adversary.

Sounds pretty serious and complicated!

Thankfully, God has made things much simpler for us. He has given us a powerful weapon for a purpose: to create or destroy. A weapon that is so potent; it can bring forth either life or death, depending on how you use it.

No, it's not a gun, it's your tongue! Believe it or not, your tongue is more effective than any other weapon ever created!

"Death and life are in the power of the tongue: and they that love it shall eat the fruit thereof." (Proverbs 18:21)

One word can affect your daughter's life forever, in other words!

"So shall my word be that goeth forth out of my mouth: it shall not return unto me void, but it shall accomplish that which I please, and it shall prosper in the thing whereto I sent it." (Isaiah 55:11)

Now, there is a close correlation between your tongue and a gun in that once a word leaves your mouth, just like a bullet shot from the chamber of a gun, you can't stop it, nor can you take it back! Most importantly, more often than not, it will hit its intended target!

Mothers, a real-life bullet wound, can heal over time, and in some cases, even be forgotten. But a single hurtful word from your mouth to your daughter has the potential to live forever as a permanent wound in her heart. That is a "deadly" serious matter, so, please, use your tongue — the most powerful weapon in the world — wisely!

The Power of a Mother's Word

"In the beginning was the Word, and the Word was with God, and the Word was God." (John 1:1)

According to Scripture, the Word was with God and the Word was God. The Word of God created everything that's ever existed. Simply put, the Word is the very beginning, the origin, of all creation!

If you desire something that appears outside of your reach, then, you must ask for it, using God's Word as your Foundation and "Backup." All you have to do is say and believe whatever it is that God has already stated concerning what you desire. Then, once you've asked, you only move forward in faith, continuing to do the will of God until you see His Word manifested.

"Ask, and it shall be given you; seek, and ye shall find; knock, and it shall be opened unto you." (Matthew 7:7)

Once you do this, you are in a position to co-create new experiences and miracles in your life!

Whenever I'm working with mothers and daughters, I make a point to tell them that their words have the power inside them. I can't overstate it: Words are too powerful to be taken lightly!

When your daughter was born, and you first looked into her eyes, you probably ever-so-gently spoke to her, right? Those words that you spoke marked the beginning of your bonding process with her. If you spoke loving words, she instantly felt loved. And if you were somehow bitter enough to speak unloving words to her, she no doubt felt unloved.

Remember, Mothers — you are your daughter's first human contact, once she's left heaven as a present sent down to you from God! When God gifted her to you, His expectation was that you would consult Him on how to properly nurture and care for her. In other words, He expects you to deal with her according to His plans for her life.

Just like Jesus had to consult the Father for instructions, so we mothers have to ask regularly of God concerning our daughters!

Realize that God has already given us the words we are to use to get His best results for our daughters. Never forget that she is His daughter first, and He sent her to the earth to serve and advance His Kingdom, not yours!

God's Word tells us that He is careful to watch over His words to perform them. He selects His words very carefully before speaking them, and everything He promises, He performs. The Bible essentially is a training manual, designed to teach us what we need to know to live our best lives in Christ — right now!

Whenever we pray or make a request of God, it's Jesus who presents our claims in heaven, before the Father. The Father then communicates the answer to the request through His already-spoken Word; Jesus then takes the answer from God's Word and speaks it to your spirit.

Suddenly, you have your answer — and maybe even your miracle!

Mothers, the lesson here is this: We must select our words carefully before speaking them, concerning any matter. None of us should just say whatever we think. However, we believe it. Rather, we should consult Jesus on the matter first, and allow Him time to ask the Father. Then, He can get back to us with the proper, Godly answer. The answer will result in a revelatory, "miracle solution" to our problem or situation, each and every time!

The words you speak to and over your daughter will affect her outcome, most assuredly. Your little girl also believes everything you say, too, until she grows old enough to recognize untruth when she hears it, at least. At that point, she'll start noting and remembering all the times she heard you tell a lie, using them as a comparison to everything she hears you say after that. Then, around the age of thirteen or so, she'll begin to question seriously, and even doubt, what you tell her!

Her distrust will likely cause you to feel challenged or threatened by her, so you might argue with her, or even punish her. You may even start to feel so insecure about your position in her life at that point, that you fear you're losing control. It is just one of the possible beginnings of classic mother-daughter conflict!

When your daughter is young, you can punish her, or either send her to her room, as you mentally try to "settle" whatever issue is between the two of you. When she gets older, your hollow words and stories that you've told her will start to demand accountability. Your daughter will desire and expect honesty from you; she'll want your genuine, factual answers! The reason that you're experiencing conflict with her in this instance is relatively straightforward. You haven't been honest and proper with her and the two of you are now long overdue for an "Honesty" conversation that produces real, clear answers… the TRUTH, in other words!

Every time you avoid having an honest conversation with your daughter, she trusts you less. As, I said earlier, her questioning of you possibly will begin around age thirteen. If you don't deal with the issues at hand, she'll eventually mature to twenty-three, thirty-three, forty-three, then fifty-three — and you, Mother, will be around age seventy-three, or so — and the two of you will still not have had that honest conversation!

Perhaps you figured that the passage of time would take care of those things; that it would erase the need for an honest dialogue from your daughter's memory. Time passes, for certain, but this doesn't mean it allows us to ignore our issues. Time doesn't take care of what's been broken or left unspoken. That's the job of the mother and daughter involved!

So now, after decades of unnecessary silence surrounding your "issues," you're wondering why your daughter doesn't want to take care of you when you're now eighty-three years old and needing personalized care. Well, it's because she doesn't know you, or she strongly resents you!

Will the real mother please stand up, and tell the truth to her daughter — before years and years have passed, and it's nearly too late?!

Your little girl has been waiting nearly all her life to hear the real truth from your heart, and you've spent that same amount of time hoping things will somehow magically resolve on their own, or simply just go away! But I'm here to tell you that they won't. Your negative words have finally caught up with you, and you have no choice now if you want a better relationship with your daughter. You must face the truth and tell the truth!

Thankfully, in light of all this, I have some Good News for you...

Mother, again, it is never too late to have that honest conversation with your daughter. You don't want to die and leave her with negative thoughts or unresolved issues concerning you. As was said, such negative experiences and feelings have the potential to hold her captive for the rest of her life, and the life of her daughter!

Mother, your spoken truth is the key to unlocking your daughter's troubled mind and heart and setting her free. Through your very words, you have the power to affect her release!

Here's a tried-and-true technique, designed to break the ice and start the process of reconnecting your hearts:

First, take your daughter's hands into yours and look straight in her eyes for thirty seconds. Don't do any talking or moving. Just look deep into her eyes!

Next, relax for three seconds.

Now, look straight into her eyes again for another thirty seconds. Again, don't do any talking or moving. Look into her eyes until you feel her spirit! When you begin to feel her energy, keep looking, go deeper!

At this point, one or both of you may start to cry. This reaction is pretty typically, actually, so feel free to let the tears flow — they're just an indication that a breakthrough is near! Don't break your eye contact: hold it, hold it, hold it!
When you get your breakthrough, give each other a heartfelt HUG!

Next, proceed to apologize to your daughter, Mother, for anything that you may have said or done to hurt her, in any way. Don't worry about the details and specifics of what you've done — only apologize in general, overall, but do it with sincerity!
Your daughter might take a deep breath and start to cry at this point, too, recognizing that she has been waiting for this moment for many years, and it has finally arrived!

Next, tell your daughter that you love her, Mother, and let her know you are ready and willing to answer any questions she wants to ask you. Be compliant and be honest, because she may just ask you some tough questions. Also, remember that words are very powerful; choose yours in response to hers, carefully!

After you have had your first session of your honest conversation, plan a session a week to continue the process.

A Mother and Daughter's Ultimate Weapon

Special note: Listening and Respect is the key elements in this process.

The two of you should now make plans to spend at least one hour a week on a mother-daughter date of some kind! This quality time together will allow your spirits to reconnect, forging and strengthening your bond.

Mother, I can't stress enough that your words have ultimate renewing power in your relationship with your daughter! So, please use loving words.

Going back to that earlier example, let's just say you're now eighty-three years old, and God decides to grant you another ten years of life. I can almost guarantee that your final decade will be your best one ever, having a renewed, restored, and honest relationship with your daughter!

Now that there's restored love and trust between you and your daughter, your daughter will be more willing to help and assist you, given that she's finally feeling your unhindered love toward her and your genuine concern for her feelings. The power of the right words can indeed renew any relationship gone wrong!

Keep in mind, Mother, and this goes for you, too, Daughter: You were created in the image of God to become all that you can imagine. All you've got to do is say it, and you can have the mother-daughter relationship of your dreams!

Consider, too, to only say what you want to see manifested in your relationship. Because what you say, is what you'll get!

"Pleasant words are as an honeycomb, sweet to the soul, and health to the bones." (Proverbs 16:24)

The Importance of Our Thoughts

Words create our thoughts. And it's our thoughts that propel us mentally, forward — or backward — on this journey called life!

Thoughts are very powerful indeed. They determine what we see within our mind's eye. Both what we see and what we think we see help influence the decisions we make. Thoughts, in other words, are actual, existing things!

We all have both positive and negative thoughts. And it's the "conflict" between these two types of thoughts that create the confrontations within our minds. Thoughts also control our intra-conversations; the negative ones have a tendency to leave us feeling very confused like we just don't know what to do! When this is the case, every time you try to make a decision, it seems, your thoughts present a conflicting argument, and if you listen too long to those opposing ideas, you'll likely end up right back where you started!

Sometimes, to try to figure out what to do, we pull out an old playing card; "Let me call my girlfriend and see what she thinks." But it's not your girlfriend that has the answer that you need. And when it comes to certain family and friends, in particular, most of the time they won't have the right answer!

The truth is that all your answers are right inside of you. Why? Because God made you with all that you would ever need to live a loving, healthy, and prosperous life here on earth! All you have to do is call on Him, ask Him in the name of Jesus and He will answer you! Try Him out. Take a chance and pull out that card! In fact, I encourage you to make Jesus your very best friend. Go to Him first when it comes to your questions and problems. I guarantee that if you believe in Him and His promises, He'll answer you! His Word promises:

"If any of you lack wisdom, let him ask of God, that giveth to all men liberally, and upbraideth not; and it shall be given him." (James 1:5)

Thankfully, you can control your thoughts, using the Word of God. Not using your words and techniques — they simply aren't that reliable — but again, only the Word of God! That is why Jesus said, *"For I have not spoken of myself; but the Father which sent me, He gave me a commandment, what I should say, and what I should speak." (John 12:49)*
Bottom line, if you don't control your thoughts, your thoughts will control you!

Thoughts are like a carousel. They go around and around, around and around in your mind, until you finally give them your full attention. Negative thoughts, especially, rarely just go away on their own. You have to banish them through the Word of God!

If you don't give your thoughts your focus and attention,

they will remain in your subconscious mind and replay themselves over and over, until you feel you just can't take them anymore!

Your old thoughts just want to have an honest conversation with you. As they watch the long line of new thoughts entering into your mind on a constant basis, it's like they're wondering when their turn is going to come! They're just waiting for you to make a decision about them, one way or the other, so they can move either on or out, so to speak.

Thoughts may also serve as a preview to a forthcoming vision. The Word of God says:

"For as he thinketh in his heart, so is he..." (Proverbs 23:7)

"For my thoughts are not your thoughts, neither are your ways my ways, saith the LORD." (Isaiah 55:8)

"O LORD, how great are thy works! and thy thoughts are very deep." (Psalm 92:5)

"The LORD knoweth the thoughts of man, that they are vanity." (Psalm 94:11)

"Search me, O God, and know my heart: try me, and know my thoughts..." (Psalm 139:23)

"Commit thy works unto the LORD, and thy thoughts shall be established." (Proverbs 16:3)

Learn how to manage your thoughts by transforming your mind. Think only of good things, for as much as possible. The more you think about good things, the easier it becomes to manage your thoughts. We are creatures of habit, with the God-given ability to transform our minds until we transform ourselves — into who we want to be!

If we see something or someone we admire, for example, we might immediately choose to copy the style and make it our own. The media is used to giving us "visuals" and influencing our tastes for the latest trends and styles, to the extent that you can easily see when a certain product, hairstyle, fashion, or beauty trend is catching on. That is until the next trend comes along to replace it!

I especially like to use fashion and beauty trends as an example when it comes to my female clients because the majority of them pay pretty close attention to what they wear and how they wear it; women tend to be very concerned with how they look. So if we see an appealing hairstyle or nail color, for example, we will quickly decide whether to adopt it for ourselves. Some way, somehow, sometimes even regardless of the financial budget we're on; we will find a way to meet the expense of that new hairstyle or manicure!

The point I'm making here is the ease and speed with which we're able to make a decision about something when we feel sure of it. When it comes to the things we want most in life, decision-making is usually not a chore, because we're choosing the things that make us feel good!

There are so many things, good and bad, that can affect our lives in a single day. So whenever you happen upon something that makes you feel good, it's typical to make a decision just to go with it, often out of a need to relieve some of the life's stress! Ultimately, it's because of the power and influence of our thoughts that Jesus tells us, "Only think of good things." Thinking on good things brings peace to your mind, joy to your heart, and rest to your soul!

"Finally, brethren, whatsoever things are true, whatsoever things are honest, whatsoever things are just, whatsoever things are pure, whatsoever things are lovely, whatsoever things are of good report; if there be any virtue, and if there be any praise, think on these things." (Philippians 4:8)

If you find yourself thinking about things that are not true, not honest, not just, not pure, not lovely, and not of a good report, don't think about them any longer!

They will only bring you stress and move you out of the will of God. It's God's will that your body enjoy peace and tranquility. So if you're feeling stressed, it's because you've moved your mind out of the present will of God!

God is a peaceful Spirit, and you are made in His image. So if you are not of a peaceful spirit, you've apparently made a decision to go against His will, somewhere in your life. In your state of unrest and lack of peace, in other words, you're only experiencing the life of your choosing, your thoughts.

The Good News is that you can make another decision. You can decide to experience the lifestyle that God created for you. It's a life comprised of love, hope, peace, joy, and happiness!

Now, doesn't that sound GOOD?

The Importance of Our Visions

When we hear the word vision, most of us think of the obvious: eyesight!

Eyesight is what allows us visual access to the physical world. Spiritual sight, on the other hand, allows us access to the spiritual world.

Too many mothers rear their daughters from their physical eyesight; they go according to what they see and understand in the natural world. But recognize, Mothers, that God expects you to rear your daughter using your spiritual sight. For it's your spiritual sight that connects you to His will and plan for both you and your daughter.

Using your spiritual sight requires trusting God, however. It means making Him your personal GPS because He's your navigator, you shouldn't ever leave home without Him!
Imagine yourself driving a car in an unfamiliar territory. It's dark, and the spirit of fear is starting to creep into your mind. You don't see anyone that you can ask for directions, and you're beginning to see the same street signs over and over. Now you're scared! So you begin to pray.

"Lord, I'm lost, and I am scared," you whisper. "Please help me!"

That's when you hear that familiar internal voice, so still

and calm, saying, "Use your GPS." And you go, "Wow, I didn't even think of that. I completely forgot I had a GPS!"

Mothers, this is similar to what happens during times when we find ourselves lost, confused, fearful, or full of doubt concerning our daughters and how we're parenting them. Sometimes as a mother, you just don't know which direction to take, what decision to make or who you can even ask!

Maybe you have sought others' advice, talking to every responsible person within your reach. Their suggestions might have been sound enough, but you may still find yourself sitting with your head hung low, saying with a sigh, "Lord, I just don't know what else to do!"

It's at that moment that you need to shut off your natural eyesight and tune into your spiritual vision. Once you do, you'll hear that still small voice reminding you to "Use your GPS."

Next, your intra-conversations will probably turn up the volume. You'll find yourself asking, "A GPS? How can that help me with my problems?"

Then, that still, small voice replies, "I'm not referring to your Global Positioning Satellite. I'm talking about your **God Protection System!**"

In case you didn't already know, your "God Protection System" is always with you. All you have to do is speak to it, have faith in it, and watch it work! It will take you straight to the godly solution to any problem you encounter — with your daughter, or otherwise!

Trust the Holy Spirit, which is the voice behind your internal GPS. He has the answers to all your questions. Wouldn't you agree that that's some incredibly *Good News* — the knowledge that there's an answer to every question, and all you need to do is ask to receive it?!

"And I say unto you, Ask, and it shall be given you; seek, and ye shall find; knock, and it shall be opened unto you. For every one that asketh receiveth; and he that seeketh findeth; and to him that knocketh it shall be opened." (Luke 11:9-10)

Our spiritual visions also serve as "intra-previews," from God of things to come in our lives.

Because God is a spirit, we must go within ourselves — using the access given to us by Jesus Christ, who lives inside us — to communicate with Him. In addition to being our means of spiritual access to God, Jesus also is our advocate before God.

You also must remember to use your faith. Believe that you've received! Remember what the Word says:

"For we walk by faith, not by sight." (II Corinthians 5:7)

When it comes to God, your only option is to believe in His Word. Then and only then will He release His promises and blessings in your life!

The Reality of Truth

What does "reality" mean to you? Think about it a minute. For me, reality has to do with the truth of the matter.

For example, when you stand in front of a mirror and take a look at your body, you get a general idea of what it is other people see when they look at you. Right? And while you're standing there looking at yourself, you'll probably end up looking into your own eyes, as well, which will give you a momentary glimpse into your spirit.

Most mothers and daughters tend to avoid talking about their "reality," or the nature of what they look like, spiritually speaking, to each other, and how they make each other feel. They also fail to acknowledge the beauty and power of the God-given spirit within them.

Most of us know that the spirit is within us, because it "speaks" to us constantly, day in and day out. We do consult with it every day, as we go about making daily decisions. We may even find ourselves debating with it from time to time, but either way, we have to come to some conclusion in the end and make peace with our inner-selves. For it is impossible to make any decision outside of you consulting with your spirit, through your intra-conversations!

There's just no getting around it: You're a spiritual being, living in a natural body, having a dual human being/spirit-being experience!

Because we can see both our bodies and other human bodies more easily than we can others' inner spirits, we tend to pay more attention to the body, than to the spirit. The spirit is something that you can't see with your natural eye, yet it happens to be the "real you" of every human being. It's the part of each one of us that will live forever if we allow our souls to accept Jesus as Lord and Savior.

Your spirit is inside your body for protection, and to permit your spirit full access to the things in the natural realm. Your spirit is the one thing that can never be touched by human hands. It came here in the purest of forms, and it will return to God in its pure state. Your spirit came within a seed that entered your mother, by your natural father. But it was your spiritual Father, God, who allowed the miracle of your conception to take place. It was God's plan and design to have babies carried and birthed by mothers (as opposed to fathers), and as I've said countless times, God holds the mother personally responsible for the outcome of His daughter.

"AS IS THE MOTHER, SO IS HER DAUGHTER." (EZEKIEL 16:44)

The mother has nine months to prepare the mind and spirit of her unborn daughter for her pending birth. During those nine months, whatever the mother eats, drinks, says, thinks, sees, or feels, directly affects the temperament of her daughter. Mother, if you enjoyed a peaceful pregnancy, your daughter will likely have a peaceful temperament. If on the other hand, you experienced a frustrating nine months, your daughter may just have a "frustrating" temperament when she finally arrives!

God gave you Mother, a clean, unblemished spirit/daughter, and made her in His image. You, therefore, are held responsible for ensuring that the spirit of your daughter remains similarly clean and unblemished.

Your reality is a reflection of your state of mind, and of your relationship with God. It's not so much about what you see in the natural world, or what happens to you in the physical realm; rather, it's about whether your final resting place will be Heaven or Hell. The two choices each of us has are called LIFE and DEATH. We get to choose the one we want!

"I call heaven and earth to witness against you today, which I have set before you life and death, blessing and curse.

"Therefore choose life, that you and your offspring may live." (Deuteronomy 30:19)

Wow, God just gave us a pretty strong hint there: "Choose life," He says!

If you don't like where you are in life, simply change what you say. Because...

"YOUR WORDS CREATE YOUR THOUGHTS; YOUR THOUGHTS CREATE YOUR VISIONS, AND YOUR VISIONS CREATE YOUR REALITY!"
-DR. BESSIE FLETCHER

Chapter Eleven

Mothers and Daughters: The Complete Package

Mother and Daughter Health

As we discussed, too many mothers tend to pay more attention to the outside of their bodies than the insides especially if they're worried about having put on extra pounds!

God's health plan begins from within and it progresses outward. Good health must be a part of every mother's belief system and practice, and her daughter's, as well, once she reaches a certain age of understanding. Remember, as a man or woman thinks, so is he/she. If you think you are sick, then, you are sick! Likewise, if you think you are healthy and whole, you are healthy and whole.

So, what is it that you're currently thinking — and saying — about your health? Do you ever make statements like:
- I always get a headache on the weekends!
- She makes me sick!
- My mother had heart trouble, and my sister did, too, so I just know I'm going to have it one day because it runs in my family!

Tell me, does it run in your family or does it run in your mouth?

Remember, **You Have What You Say!**

When it comes to what we speak about our health, we must say and confess only what God says about the matter. The power to heal is the Word of God. The reason so many mothers and daughters suffer illness is because they're listening to the words of others, and not the words of the One who created them! Wouldn't you think that the One who created you knows best how to repair you? Think about that for a moment!

"Then shall thy light break forth as the morning, and thine health shall spring forth speedily: and thy righteousness shall go before thee; the glory of the LORD shall be thy reward." (Isaiah 58:8)

"Beloved, I wish above all things that thou mayest prosper and be in health, even as thy soul prospereth." (III John 1:2)

Mother and Daughter Peace

God's version of peace is the only kind available for the world. His original intent was for all of us to love each other and to get along, but as you well know if you've read the Bible, there are plenty cases where His children, just didn't get along!

Such situations — of conflict, strife, and unrest — always resulted in fear and distrust among God's children. And that disturbed God's peace!

The peace of God was disturbed, for example, when Adam and Eve disobeyed His instructions regarding the Tree of the Knowledge of Good and Evil. They were given specific instructions on what to do on a daily basis, including what to eat and what not to eat, or even touch. Once they violated God's instructions, it not only brought an end to their peace and tranquility, it bothered God, too! Their sinful, disobedient actions completely disrupted the peaceful paradise that was the Garden of Eden. The animals that they used to play with and enjoy so freely suddenly became their worst nightmare!

Mothers and daughters, the story of Adam and Eve's sin serves as a prime example of why you might be experiencing a lack of peace in your life today. When you are out of order and out of sync with the will of God, you simply cannot rest. You'll want to go to sleep, but the sleep just won't be peaceful. You may even take a sleeping pill to help get you there faster, but you won't be able to get a good night's rest until you get back in line with the Word of God!

Peace is something you simply cannot buy or barter; it's a gift from God. And once you align your mind, body, and soul with His Word, His peace is automatically granted to you. When God's peace is upon you, nothing can disturb your flow. The world may be experiencing its craziness, but what's happening outside will not come near you or your family!
God's Word says:

"*I have said these things to you, that in me you may have peace. In the world you will have tribulation. But take heart; I have overcome the world.*" (John 16:33)

"*When a man's ways please the LORD, he makes even his enemies to be at peace with him.*" (Proverbs 16:7)

Mothers and daughters, if you lack peace, stop and take inventory of what's happening in your personal life, your professional life, your church life, your dealings in your neighborhood or community, your close relationships, and most importantly, your relationship with God!

Somewhere in the equation, in one of the above categories, you will find your answer; usually, it's right there in front of your eyes. The Spirit of God constantly speaks to us, telling us when we're right and when we're wrong. Just think back for a moment on the times you made the wrong choice, and the Spirit of God checked you, saying, "Didn't I tell you not to do that?" (Sounds kind of like your mother, doesn't it?)

Or you just may be the one who does the talking, saying to

yourself, "Something told me not to do that!" That "something," clearly, was God.

Here are some words of peace to bless your spirit:

"...do not be anxious about anything, but in everything by prayer and supplication with thanksgiving let your requests be made known to God. And the peace of God, which surpasses all understanding, will guard your hearts and your minds in Christ Jesus." (Philippians 4:6-7)

"Blessed are the peacemakers, for they shall be called sons of God." (Matthew 5:9)

"How beautiful upon the mountains are the feet of him who brings good news, who publishes peace, who brings good news of happiness, who publishes salvation, who says to Zion, "Your God reigns." (Isaiah 52:7)

"May the God of peace be with you all. Amen." (Romans 15:33)

Mother and Daughter Protection

As a mother, you have a natural instinct to want to protect your daughter. If danger ever appears to get too close to her, your "defense mechanism" automatically kicks in and compels you to fight for her — to the best of your ability and with great ferocity!

Most people know that it's a dangerous thing to mess with a loving mother's daughter! A mother can grow quite sensitive when it comes to matters concerning her vulnerable daughter even when she knows her daughter is in the wrong. It doesn't matter to her, though; she'll deal with her daughter later, privately, but for the time being, her "protection mode" has taken over and she's on the counter-attack! Many mothers find that they aren't able to think very clearly when this happens — their maternal instincts and emotions have a way of overpowering their sense of reason!

In most cases, that's the point when Mom needs to walk away from the situation. She needs to take several deep breaths to calm herself, then return later to deal with the issue at hand. After she's calmed down some and realized that her daughter is not in danger, she'll be better able to listen and respond in a reasonable manner.

As mothers, it is certainly our job to protect our daughters, and that job doesn't necessarily end when they reach legal adulthood. No matter how old your daughter is, there's something inside of you that will always defend her, even to the death and usually, that's the death of whomever or whatever is bothering her!

It's the natural, God-given tendency of the mother to be as protective, nurturing, and defensive toward her daughter as possible. And if God has blessed you to be a mother, know that He also has equipped you with absolutely everything you need to be the very best mother you can be!

Just as God created you with a built-in protection sensor (Holy

Spirit) when it comes to your daughter, He has one when it comes to you! How do I know God has a protection sensor inside Him like all healthy mothers do? Because He said in His word, "Let's us make them in our image!"

As our Father, God, is the creator and source of all that is loving, concerned, and protective. That is why He sent His only begotten Son, Jesus, to save us all from the enemy of our souls.

"The Lord will keep you from all evil; he will keep your life. The Lord will keep your going out and your coming in from this time forth and forevermore." (Psalm 121:7-8)

"Fear not, for I am with you; Be not dismayed, for I am your God. I will strengthen you, Yes, I will help you, I will uphold you with My righteous right hand." (Isaiah 41:10)

"I cried unto the LORD with my voice, and he heard me out of his holy hill. Selah." (Psalms 3:4)

"Keep me, O LORD, from the hands of the wicked; preserve me from the violent man; who have purposed to overthrow my goings." (Psalms 140:4)

"I will not be afraid of ten thousands of people, that have set themselves against me round about. (Psalms 3:6)

Mother and Daughter Joy

When the evil one comes by night, joy cometh in the morning!
God promised to keep you safe and to protect you from all of

your enemies. Just knowing this should bring joy to your heart! Joy is much like peace in that you can't buy it because it's a gift from God. Isn't it amazing how God has provided you His very best, as gifts directly from Him? Thankfully, what He has for you, the world can neither give you, nor take away!

I'm sure many of you have heard something similar to this statement before. Have you ever really thought about it, though? What exactly is it that the world can't give you, or steal from you?

The answer is that the world can't give your true love, joy, peace, hope, or happiness. The world can't give these things to you because the world doesn't have them in the first place. Genuine love, joy, peace, hope, and happiness are all gifts from above, from God. And when you are walking in obedience to His Word, they're just some of the priceless gifts, benefits, blessings, and promises He bestows upon you!

If you're an older mother, remember how back in the day, whenever your daughter was obedient and followed the rules you laid down for her, it made you so pleased to be her mother? It truly made your job less stressful and more enjoyable, didn't it? It made you want to reward your daughter for her good behavior, so you would give her something that you knew would make her happy, right?

I certainly remember the joy I got whenever my daughter listened to and followed my instructions well, as well as the joy I'd experience from putting a random gift on her bed. My daughter was mostly very obedient. But if a challenging situation ever came up, I made a point to discuss it with her, and we'd come to an understanding of my expectation of her behavior from that point on. And she would rise to the occasion.

It gave me great pleasure, then, to shower her with small, unexpected gifts here and there, as a reward for being such a good daughter. When she was a youth, I recalled getting so excited when I heard her yelling about the $5 she'd just miraculously "found" on her bed! "Momma is this for me?" she'd call out from her bedroom, knowing that it obviously was. Almost before I could respond with a "Yes," she would run into the room where I was and throw her arms around me, with a genuine, "Thank you, Momma!"

Naturally, joy would flood my heart at that point, and I'd typically find myself thinking about the next thing I could "randomly" give her to make her happy, as I truly got joy! My daughter is married with children of her own, but to this day, we continue to seek out ways to surprise each other with doses of joy.

Mothers, regardless of how much joy we're able to effect in our daughters' lives, we can never come close to giving them the joy that God can! God is a jealous God, after all, and He reserves His very best gifts — those that bring ultimate, divine joy — to be given by Him alone. Hey, knowing how much it pleases you to give to your daughter, can you blame Him?

"Let them shout for joy, and be glad, that favour my

righteous cause: yea, let them say continually, Let the LORD be magnified, which hath pleasure in the prosperity of his servant." (Psalm 35:27)

"Make a joyful noise to the LORD, all the earth! Serve the LORD with gladness! Come into his presence with singing! Know that the LORD, he is God! It is he who made us, and we are his; we are his people, and the sheep of his pasture." (Psalm 100:1-3)

"Blessed is the people that know the joyful sound: they shall walk, O LORD, in the light of thy countenance." (Psalm 89:15)

"Let us come into his presence with thanksgiving; let us make a joyful noise to him with songs of praise!" (Psalm 95:2)

"And now shall mine head be lifted up above mine enemies round about me: therefore will I offer in his tabernacle sacrifices of joy; I will sing, yea, I will sing praises unto the LORD." (Psalm 27:6)

Mother and Daughter Forgiveness

Through my many years as a Christian clinical psychologist, I've unfortunately discovered that lack of forgiveness is the number one relationship killer for most mothers and daughters.

Rather frequently, either a mother or a daughter will come into my counseling session with her mind made up not to forgive her mother or daughter. I can tell this without her even articulating it by her body language, which always speaks louder than words. If she manages to bring her mother, the two of them may hardly be willing to sit next to each, as they try to avoid looking at each other. When I see these signs, I know we're all in for one interesting journey!

The mother has her reasons for coming to the counseling session, and the daughter has her reasons for bringing her mother. In most cases, if the daughter is twenty-five or younger in age, it's the mother who brings her to the session. If the daughter is older than twenty-five, on the other hand, she's usually the one that brings her mother. Whichever one had the original idea that they should seek counsel, I find that they're also usually the one wanting me to "fix" the other! Their thinking is that the other one, their mother or their daughter, is the problem in the relationship, and not they.

The point is, the need to forgive is usually quite hard for a mother or daughter to identify within themselves. Each one is looking at the other's role in the situation — what they said or did that was just plain wrong! And the one feeling the most wronged, if they're not claiming equal hurt, may have further added to the confusion by soliciting others' opinions when family members and friends don't have much to do with it, let alone the necessary tools to help resolve the situation.

The truth is that most of us, when we feel wronged, tend to seek the support of someone we know will agree with us.

Their verbal validation bringing us a measure of comfort in the situation. And if the first person we go to happens not to agree with us, we keep on searching, until we find that someone who will side with us! In such a case, the accusing mother or daughter now has her "backup" firmly in place and is ready to build her case!

Personally, I can't think of a situation that could arise where a mother or daughter could not forgive one another! Daughters, we are talking here about the woman who carried you for nine long months in her body. Then, once you got here, she clothed, fed, and took care of you, when you were unable to take care of yourself. And you mean to tell me that you can't find it in your heart to forgive such a person who sacrificed so greatly for you? Come on, now!

I've seen mothers and daughters lose anywhere from six months to thirty years' time in their relationship, simply because they decided they weren't going to forgive! I've seen situations where the mother or daughter became deathly ill, too, and as a result, forgiveness suddenly was at the heart of the one who'd been withholding it for so long. Such situations let me know that a deep love for the other remained in their heart all along.

Somehow, the unforgiving mother or daughter had created an illusion, an idea, of what they thought happened, which was probably reinforced by the opinions of others. That led to the hardening of their hearts, blinding them from acknowledging their true love for the other.

Mothers and Daughters: The Complete Package

Needless to say, there is a bond between a mother and her daughter that is unbreakable! That bond emerges in pure love. When the mother and daughter are getting along, their thoughts and hearts are healthy, and they readily acknowledge their love for one another. But if they allow negative words, lost time, and pride to stiffen their hearts toward one another, it can create a stronghold that won't allow their bond to function like it was meant to. Though they may want to undo the negative situation, they just don't know how!

To get back to the original love between them, I tell my mother-daughter clients that it starts with the mother. Mothers, go back to that exercise I suggested earlier, where you looked into your daughter's eyes for thirty seconds, then repeated it. Try this exercise more than once, for as long as you can, and eventually, you'll watch the hurt roll away. The hurt usually leaves through the expression of tears. When the tears start, simply let them flow; they are "washing clean" either you or your daughter — or hopefully, both of you— of those old, pent-up emotions that have been blocking and stifling the flow of your love toward one another. I promise you if you're brave enough to practice this technique with consistency, your emotions will melt like butter. I've used it in my counseling sessions for many years — it works every time!

I ask my clients if God can forgive you for all the wrong you've done to Him, how is it that you can't forgive your mother or daughter? It's not unusual for the client to give me a curious look at that point — a question mark on their face that essentially says, "Well, I never really thought about it that way!"

The Word of God says:

"For if you forgive others their trespasses, your heavenly Father will also forgive you, but if you do not forgive others their trespasses, neither will your Father forgive your trespasses." (Matthew 6:14-15)

"Judge not, and you will not be judged; condemn not, and you will not be condemned; forgive, and you will be forgiven..." (Luke 6:37)

"Therefore I tell you, her sins, which are many, are forgiven — for she loved much. But he who is forgiven little, loves little." (Luke 7:47)

"Then said Jesus, Father, forgive them; for they know not what they do. And they parted his raiment, and cast lots." (Luke 23:34)

God will forgive mothers and daughters of nearly every sin — including speaking against His beloved Son, Jesus (for those foolish enough to go there!). But there's one sin that can never be forgiven, according to the Word:

"And whoever speaks a word against the Son of Man will be forgiven, but whoever speaks against the Holy Spirit will not be forgiven, either in this age or in the age to come." (Matthew 12:32)

This scripture sounds a lot like that "one forbidden tree" that set before Adam and Eve in the Garden...centuries later, the entire world is still feeling the effects of their fateful decision!

Mother and Daughter Prosperity

Mothers and daughters, God wants you to know that He has blessed your health, as well as your wealth. It's His will that you be prosperous! Most of you will believe God to heal you and give you ongoing good health, but few have faith, it seems when it comes to prosperity. Some of you think prosperity is only for "them." Who is "them," the already-rich?

Prosperity is for whosoever believes in it! You can't receive what you don't believe. If you don't believe in healing, you won't receive healing. If you don't believe in money, you won't have money. The money will come into your hands, but then it'll leave faster than it came! It can't stay in a place where there is no faith for it. For that reason, it simply will keep passing through your hands, until you finally change your mindset about it.

According to the Word, Jesus died and became poor so that you could be rich!

"For ye know the grace of our Lord Jesus Christ, that though he was rich, yet for your sake he became poor, so that you by his poverty might become rich." (II Corinthians 8:9)

Maybe you didn't realize it before, but you need to take in this revelation. Because once you transform your mind, wealth and prosperity will show up in your life, money will come to live in your bank account!

Prosperity has not been taught to many of our daughters because, as mothers, we weren't taught. Most mothers heard that "money is the root of all evil!" They've heard the lie that if one has money, they can't effectively serve God. That is not what's in your bible, Mothers. Rather, the Scripture says,

"For the love of money is the root of all evil: which while some coveted after, they have erred from the faith, and pierced themselves through with many sorrows." (I Timothy 6:10)

So what exactly is prosperity?

Prosperity is sufficiency in all areas of one's life. If you are sick and have lots of money, that's not prosperity. If you are healthy and have no money, that's not prosperity. If you are healthy and have lots of money, but you have a confused mind, that's not prosperity, either!

"And God is able to make all grace abound to you, so that having all sufficiency in all things at all times, you may abound in every good work." (II Corinthians 9:8)

God's Word says:

"Beloved, I wish above all things that thou mayest prosper and be in health, even as thy soul prospereth." (III John 1:2)

Some mothers and daughters may even think that wealth is exclusively for men. But that's far from the truth. God gave many examples of mothers and daughters in the Bible who possessed great wealth.

The Queen of Sheba is a prime example of one such woman. Both a mother and a daughter, she was a beautiful, powerful, and intelligent woman, who came from royalty and was very confident in her wealth and status. She was so wealthy; in fact, that some scholars estimate that she gave away a billion dollars in gold, spices and other impressive gifts to King Solomon! And not only did she have tremendous wealth, but she had favor and influence with the king, as well.

Prosperity isn't a curse; it's a great blessing. It also is a promise from God. You can read more about it in God's Word, and when you believe it — that you will have "all sufficiency in all things" — you will begin to see it manifested in both you and your daughter's life!

Mother and Daughter Wealth

When most mothers and daughters think of prosperity, they think of wealth. Prosperity and wealth are related in definition, yet they are worlds apart in reality. Prosperity deals with your having affluence, riches, and success; wealth, on the other hand, pertains to all of the above but also has to do with your assets, capital, trusts, holdings, and other fortunes. Wealth is accumulated over generations. You may have heard the term, "old money." Well, "old money" actually can be found in the Word of God:

"In all the land were found no women as beautiful as

the daughters of Job; and their father gave them an inheritance among their brothers." (Job 42:15)

Most of us mothers weren't born into families possessing generational wealth, or old money (neither do most of us come from "new money," for that matter!), so we weren't able to raise our daughters with a "silver spoon in their mouths," as it's sometimes said. But in reality, Mothers, you and your daughter were born under God's covenant, which is even better than "coming from money"! His Word says:

"But, as it is written, 'What no eye has seen, nor ear heard, nor the heart of man imagined, what God has prepared for those who love him' "— (I Corinthians 2:9)

In other words, God has already provided you with all that you will ever need. You can have whatever you can imagine! Mother, let's say that you've prepared lunch for your daughter. You leave her a note, telling her that you left lunch in the refrigerator for her. She comes home hungry, then immediately calls you at work, asking, "Mom, is there something to eat?" You ask her if she saw the note you left her. She says, "Yes." You then ask her with concern, "Well, did you read it?" "Yes," she says again. You pause, even more, concerned now, then you finally ask, "Well, did you understand what you read?" If she replies "Yes" yet again, then you're no doubt skeptical at this point! "I don't understand the problem then," you say. "I've left you all that you need to have a satisfying, healthy meal. All you have to do is open the refrigerator, take out the lunch I've already prepared for you, and eat and enjoy it. Go ahead, it's yours!"

Mothers and daughters, this is where I suspect some of you get hung up. God has already given you all that you will ever need or desire. In other words, you need not want for anything because you already have everything! This is why the Word says:

"Therefore I tell you, do not be anxious about your life, what you will eat or what you will drink, nor about your body, what you will put on. Is not life more than food, and the body more than clothing?" (Matthew 6:25)

When you're in God, all you have to do is have the desire, and what you desire will be manifested in your life. That is what I like to call creating your own personalized Garden of Eden. It is here that you'll find your desires meeting your reality!

Once you realize that what you think you want you already have — like the daughter not taking advantage of the food her mother left her in the refrigerator — you will thank God, and enjoy the wonderful, delicious life that He's prepared for you! It's in the refrigerator. However, it's not in the freezer, so get it before it spoils because it won't necessarily last long; you can't assume it'll always be there! Again, God has set a beautiful, exciting life before you — a "healthy meal," so to speak, featuring all your favorite foods — so you might as well grab and enjoy it to the fullest. Mothers, eat, drink, and be merry and remember to share it with your daughters!

Wealth is full of infinite possibilities for the one who

possesses it. God's Word says:

"...*All things are possible for one who believes.*" *(Mark 9:23)*

Wealth is first created within the mind. You must first believe in wealth before you can receive wealth. Like money, wealth simply will keep on moving until it finds a house that's made of faith!

"...*Have faith in God.*" *(Mark 11:22)*

"*But without faith it is impossible to please Him, for he who comes to God must believe that He is, and that he is a rewarder of those who diligently seek Him.*" *(Hebrews 11:6)*

I leave you with a question to consider: **What are you currently experiencing in *your* personal Garden of Eden?**

Chapter Twelve

In Conclusion...

This book was born out the age-old desire that mothers have been voicing for years, "If only there were a "Book" that could teach you how to raise your children?"

God wants mothers and daughters to know that whenever He creates something, whether it's a bird, a beast, or a human being, He supplies its every need. That obviously includes mothers and daughters. He wants you to know that there is nothing you will ever need or want to know that isn't yours already, right now!

I can't tell you how many times I've heard the above comment about there being no go-to manual for mothers to rear their daughters. I sometimes even get the sense that the mother blames God for this, for supposedly not giving her instructions on how to raise a perfect daughter!

And of course, I had the same concern and complaint when I was a young mother.

As a daughter, you grow up watching your mother and

how she does things, and you make mental notes all along about certain things you like and dislike, and how you plan to do things differently when it's your turn to be a mother. Daughters create a mental picture of the type of mother they wish to be, and most often, it varies quite a bit from the image of their mother!

Still somehow, the daughter finds herself, years later, living out the words of God when He said:

"As is the Mother, so is her Daughter." (Ezekiel 16:44)

From the beginning of time, God prepared the answer for every situation that you would encounter as a mother and a daughter. He said, "Seek and you shall find"! And where you should seek, Mothers and daughters, is in the Holy Bible, as it contains every answer you'll ever need.

God wants you to know that He loves you and that you are the apple of His eyes! He shared with me a few thoughts on mother-daughter relationships and how important it is for us to love one another. This book is just a small collection of His divinely-inspired thoughts.

Mothers, God wants you to know and understand His Will for your life, then teach it to your daughter, as she will, in turn, teach it to her daughter.

What is God's will for your life? His Word says:

"But seek first the kingdom of God and His righteousness, and all these things shall be added to you." (Matthew 6:33)

God wants you to trust Him, have faith in Him, and seek Him concerning all matters in your life!

In Conclusion...

Final Thoughts

1. *"In the beginning was the Word, and the Word was with God, and the Word was God." (John 1:1)*
   Do you believe that? Yes or No?

2. God created heaven and earth ... with His words!
   Do you believe that? Yes or No?

3. In this book, God made it clear to you the extent of His love for mothers and daughters.
   Do you believe that? Yes or No?

If you answered yes to any one of the above questions, I'd like to close by asking you a final one:
Which do you choose today: LIFE___ or DEATH___?

If you chose "Life", make sure you pray the Prayer of Salvation. If you haven't already, then ask God to give you the gift of the Holy Spirit.

Now, being that you are saved, consider reading this book again so that you can receive still greater revelations from it, through the Holy Spirit!

If you were saved before you read this book but didn't have the Holy Spirit, now that you've asked God to give His Spirit to you, you're better equipped to read this book with understanding, so read it again! The Greater revelation comes when the Holy Spirit is present.

Keep in mind, Mothers: God wants you to be both saved and Spirit-filled so that you can effectively lead your daughter to salvation and the way of holiness, and so that she will one day lead her daughter. You don't want to be like the five foolish virgins, do you?

The Parable of the Ten Virgins

"Then the kingdom of heaven will be like ten virgins who took their lamps and went to meet the bridegroom. Five of them were foolish, and five were wise. For when the foolish took their lamps, they took no oil with them, but the wise took flasks of oil with their lamps. As the bridegroom was delayed, they all became drowsy and slept. But at midnight there was a cry, Here is the bridegroom! Come out to meet him. Then all those virgins rose and trimmed their lamps. And the foolish said to the wise, Give us some of your oil, for our lamps are going out. But the wise answered, saying, Since there will not be enough for us and for you, go rather to the dealers and buy for yourselves. And while they were going to buy, the bridegroom came, and those who were ready went in with him to the marriage feast, and the door was

In Conclusion...

shut. Afterward, the other virgins came also, saying, 'Lord, lord, open to us.' But he answered, 'Truly, I say to you, I do not know you.' Watch therefore, for you know neither the day nor the hour." (Matthew 25:1-13)

Mothers and daughters, you don't want to miss Jesus when He returns! Once you've accepted Him as Lord and Savior, continue to walk faithfully with Him for the rest of your days, and your life will be forever abundantly blessed!

Final Nuggets

I've found only two Biblical mother-daughter stories, and only one about a mother-in-law/daughter-in-law relationship.

Mother-Daughter Stories:
1. The Canaanite Woman and Her Daughter
2. Herodias and Her Daughter

These were two vastly different types of mothers. Check them out!

Mother-In-Law/Daughter-In-Law Story:
1. Naomi and Ruth

A Mother's Cry

The Faith of the Canaanite Woman

"And Jesus went away from there and withdrew to the district of Tyre and Sidon. And behold, a Canaanite woman from that region came out and was crying, 'Have mercy on me, O Lord, Son of David; my daughter is severely oppressed by a demon.' But he did not answer her a word. And his disciples came and begged him, saying, 'Send her away, for she is crying out after us.' He answered, 'I was sent only to the lost sheep of the house of Israel.' But she came and knelt before him, saying, 'Lord, help me.' And he answered, 'It is not right to take the children's bread and throw it to the dogs.' She said, 'Yes, Lord, yet even the dogs eat the crumbs that fall from their masters' table.' Then Jesus answered her, 'O woman, great is your faith! Be it done for you as you desire.' And her daughter was healed instantly." (Matthew 15:21-28)

A Mother's Deadly Thoughts

The Influence of Herodias on Her Daughter

"For it was Herod who had sent and seized John and bound him in prison for the sake of Herodias, his brother Philip's wife, because he had married her. For, John had been saying to Herod, 'It is not lawful for you to have your brother's wife.' And Herodias had a grudge against him and wanted to put him to

In Conclusion...

death. But she could not, for Herod feared John, knowing that he was a righteous and holy man, and he kept him safe. When he heard him, he was greatly perplexed, and yet he heard him gladly. But an opportunity came when Herod on his birthday gave a banquet for his nobles and military commanders and the leading men of Galilee. For when Herodias's daughter came in and danced, she pleased Herod and his guests. And the king said to the girl, 'Ask me for whatever you wish, and I will give it to you.' And he vowed to her, 'Whatever you ask me, I will give you, up to half of my kingdom.' And she went out and said to her mother, 'For what should I ask?' And she said, 'The head of John the Baptist.' And she came in immediately with haste to the king and asked, saying, 'I want you to give me at once the head of John the Baptist on a platter.' And the king was exceedingly sorry, but because of his oaths and his guests he did not want to break his word to her. And immediately the king sent an executioner with orders to bring John's head. He went and beheaded him in the prison and brought his head on a platter and gave it to the girl, and the girl gave it to her mother. When his disciples heard of it, they came and took his body and laid it in a tomb." (Mark 6:17-29)

I Will Never Leave You
The Story of Ruth

Naomi Widowed

"In the days when the judges ruled there was a famine in the land, and a man of Bethlehem in Judah went to sojourn in the country of Moab, he and his wife and his two sons. The name of the man was Elimelech and the name of his wife Naomi, and the names of his two sons were Mahlon and Chilion. They were Ephrathites from Bethlehem in Judah. They went into the country of Moab and remained there. But Elimelech, the husband of Naomi, died, and she was left with her two sons. These took Moabite wives; the name of the one was Orpah and the name of the other Ruth. They lived there about ten years, and both Mahlon and Chilion died, so that the woman was left without her two sons and her husband."

Ruth's Loyalty to Naomi

"Then she arose with her daughters-in-law to return from the country of Moab, for she had heard in the fields of Moab that the LORD had visited his people and given them food. So she set out from the place where she was with her two daughters-in-law, and they went on the way to return to the land of Judah. But Naomi said to her two daughters-in-law, 'Go, return each of you to her mother's house. May the LORD deal kindly with you, as you have dealt with the dead and with me. The LORD grant

In Conclusion...

that you may find rest, each of you in the house of her husband!' Then she kissed them, and they lifted up their voices and wept. And they said to her, 'No, we will return with you to your people.' But Naomi said, 'Turn back, my daughters; why will you go with me? Have I yet sons in my womb that they may become your husbands? Turn back, my daughters; go your way, for I am too old to have a husband. If I should say I have hope, even if I should have a husband this night and should bear sons, would you therefore wait till they were grown? Would you therefore refrain from marrying? No, my daughters, for it is exceedingly bitter to me for your sake that the hand of the LORD has gone out against me.' Then they lifted up their voices and wept again. And Orpah kissed her mother-in-law, but Ruth clung to her.

And she said, 'See, your sister-in-law has gone back to her people and to her gods; return after your sister-in-law.' But Ruth said, 'Do not urge me to leave you or to return from following you. For where you go I will go, and where you lodge I will lodge. Your people shall be my people, and your God my God. Where you die I will die, and there will I be buried. May the LORD do so to me and more also if anything but death parts me from you.' And when Naomi saw that she was determined to go with her, she said no more."

Naomi and Ruth Return

"So, the two of them went on until they came to Bethlehem. And when they came to Bethlehem, the whole town was stirred

because of them. And the women said, 'Is this Naomi?' She said to them, 'Do not call me Naomi; call me Mara, for the Almighty has dealt very bitterly with me. I went away full, and the LORD has brought me back empty. Why call me Naomi, when the LORD has testified against me and the Almighty has brought calamity upon me?'

So Naomi returned, and Ruth the Moabite her daughter-in-law with her, who returned from the country of Moab. And they came to Bethlehem at the beginning of barley harvest." (Ruth chapter 1. For the complete story, read Ruth chapters 2-4.)

From Orphan to Queen
The Story of Esther

The King's Banquets

"Now in the days of Ahasuerus, the Ahasuerus who reigned from India to Ethiopia over 127 provinces, in those days when King Ahasuerus sat on his royal throne in Susa, the citadel, in the third year of his reign he gave a feast for all his officials and servants. The army of Persia and Media and the nobles and governors of the provinces were before him, while he showed the riches of his royal glory and the splendor and pomp of his greatness for many days, 180 days. And when these days were completed, the king gave for all the people present in Susa the citadel, both great and small, a feast lasting for seven days in the

In Conclusion...

court of the garden of the king's palace. There were white cotton curtains and violet hangings fastened with cords of fine linen and purple to silver rods and marble pillars, and also couches of gold and silver on a mosaic pavement of porphyry, marble, mother-of-pearl and precious stones. Drinks were served in golden vessels, vessels of different kinds, and the royal wine was lavished according to the bounty of the king. And drinking was according to this edict: 'There is no compulsion.' For the king had given orders to all the staff of his palace to do as each man desired. Queen Vashti also gave a feast for the women in the palace that belonged to King Ahasuerus."

Queen Vashti's Refusal

"*On the seventh day, when the heart of the king was merry with wine, he commanded Mehuman, Biztha, Harbona, Bigtha and Abagtha, Zethar and Carkas, the seven eunuchs who served in the presence of King Ahasuerus, to bring Queen Vashti before the king with her royal crown, in order to show the peoples and the princes her beauty, for she was lovely to look at. But Queen Vashti refused to come at the king's command delivered by the eunuchs. At this the king became enraged, and his anger burned within him. Then the king said to the wise men who knew the times (for this was the king's procedure toward all who were versed in law and judgment, the men next to him being Carshena, Shethar, Admatha, Tarshish, Meres, Marsena, and Memucan, the seven princes of Persia and Media, who* saw the king's face, and sat first in the kingdom): 'According to the law, what is to be done to Queen Vashti, because she has not performed the command of King Ahasuerus delivered by the eunuchs?' Then Memucan said in the presence of the king and the officials, 'Not only against the king has Queen Vashti done wrong, but also against all the officials and all the peoples who are in all the provinces of King Ahasuerus. For the queen's behavior will be made known to all women, causing them to look at their husbands with contempt, since they will say, 'King Ahasuerus commanded Queen Vashti to be brought before him, and she did not come.' This very day the noble women of Persia and Media who have heard of the queen's behavior will say the same to all the king's officials, and there will be contempt and wrath in plenty. If it please the king, let a royal order go out from him, and let it be written among the laws of the Persians and the Medes so that it may not be repealed, that Vashti is never again to come before King Ahasuerus. And let the king give her royal position to another who is better than she. So when the decree made by the king is proclaimed throughout all his kingdom, for it is vast, all women will give honor to their husbands, high and low alike.' This advice pleased the king and the princes, and the king did as Memucan proposed. He sent letters to all the royal provinces, to every province in its own script and to every people in its own language, that every man be master in his own household and speak according to the language of his people." (Esther 1. For the complete story, read Esther 2-10.)

In Conclusion...

Mothers and Daughters Who Personally Interacted with Jesus

Mary – Jesus' mother (Luke 2:41-52)

Mary and Martha – Jesus' friends; He raised their brother from the dead (Matthew 26:6-13; Mark 14:3-9; Luke 10:38-42)

Mary Magdalene – Jesus' friend; a disciple of Jesus and an apostle (Matthew 27:56; Mark 15:40; Luke 8:1-3)

Samaritan Woman – at the well, Jesus gave her Living Water (John 4:1-42)

Mother-in-law of Peter – Jesus healed her (Matthew 8:14-15; Mark 1:30-31; Luke 4:38-39)

Canaanite Woman and Her Daughter – Jesus healed the daughter (Matthew 15:21-28; Mark 7:24-30)

Menstruating Woman – she was healed by touching the hem of Jesus' garment (Mark 5:25-34)

Crippled Woman – Jesus healed her (Luke 13:10-17)

Adulterous Woman – Jesus forgave her (John 7:53, 8:11)

Widow with the Mites – she gave two mites, and Jesus said she had "given more than all the rest, because she gave all that she had" (Mark 12:41-44; Luke 21:1-4)

Anna the Prophetess – a disciple of Jesus (Luke 2:36-38)

Sinner Woman – she anointed Jesus' feet with ointment and with her tears (Luke 7:36-50)

Mary of Bethany – she anointed Jesus' head with ointment. (Matthew 26:6-13; Mark 14:3-9; John12:18)

Joanna and Susanna – two of Jesus' female disciples (Luke 8:1-3)

Widow of Nain – Jesus raised her son from the dead (Luke 7:11-17)

Daughter of Jairus – Jesus healed her (Matthew 9:18; Mark 5:35-43)

Persistent Widow – Jesus avenged her of her adversary (Luke 18:1-8)

In Conclusion...

A Good Mother Will Stand By Her Child's Side... To the Very End!

"But, standing by the cross of Jesus were his mother and his mother's sister, Mary the wife of Clopas, and Mary Magdalene. When Jesus saw his mother and the disciple whom he loved standing nearby, he said to his mother, 'Woman, behold, your son!' Then he said to the disciple, 'Behold, your mother!' And from that hour the disciple took her to his own home. After this, Jesus, knowing that all was now finished, said (to fulfill the Scripture), 'I thirst.' A jar full of sour wine stood there, so they put a sponge full of the sour wine on a hyssop branch and held it to his mouth. When Jesus therefore had received the vinegar, he said, It is finished: and he bowed his head, and gave up the ghost." (John 19:25-30)

Mother and Daughter Myrrh-Bearers for Jesus

These women helped prepare Jesus' body for burial. They witnessed his life and teachings, and were among the first to witness His empty tomb following His resurrection! (Matthew 27:55-61, 28:1-10; Mark 15:40; John 19:38, 20:18-20)

Mary (mother of Jesus)
Mary Magdalene (close friend of Jesus)

Mary (wife of Cleopas)
Martha of Bethany (sister of Lazarus)
Mary of Bethany (sister of Lazarus)
Joanna, wife of Chuza (steward of Herod Antipas)
Salome, mother of James and John (the sons of Zebedee)

Mothers and Daughters at the Resurrection of Jesus

While scholars believe there were other women present at the Resurrection, these are the ones we know by name.

Mary (mother of Jesus)
Mary Magdalene (Friend of Jesus)
Salome (mother of James and John) (not the daughter of Herodias)
Joanna (disciple of Jesus)

Mothers and Daughters at the Ascension of Jesus

While scholars believe there were other women present at the Ascension, these are the ones we know by name.
Mary (mother of Jesus)
Mary Magdalene (Friend of Jesus)
Salome (mother of James and John) (not the daughter of Herodias)
Joanna (disciple of Jesus)

In Conclusion...

GOOD NEWS!

Good News is words that make you feel good!
Good News has faith to believe God's Word!
Good News is having good health to enjoy your life here on earth!
Good News is not having to worry about what you will eat, drink or wear, or where you'll sleep!
Good News is a joy to your soul!
Good News knows no harm will come to you, your daughter, or your family!
Good News brightens up your day!
Good News erases doubt!
Good News is what Jesus Christ is all about!
Good News is the essence of The Gospels!
Good News is all about love — God loving you, as you go about loving others!
Good News is all about forgiveness — forgiving others, as you would have them forgive you!
Good News is all about trust — trusting in the Word of God!
Good News is that you have the power and authority to create your very best mother-daughter relationship, and better all other relationships in your life, as well!
Good News is that you were created to prosper!
Good News is that wealth is a part of your inheritance from God!
Good News is that your soul is being fed right now, through the

Word of God!

Good News is that God created you for His good pleasure!

Did You Know . . .
- God so loved you that He gave His only begotten Son to save you?
- Jesus died, so that you could live?
- That you are an extension of the works of Jesus Christ?
- That you are created in God's image?
- No weapon formed against you shall prosper?
- God's Word is your power?
- God's Word creates what it says?
- God wishes above all things that you have health and prosperity, even as your soul prospers?
- That by Jesus' stripes you were healed?
- That Jesus took 39 stripes for 39 diseases…all for your health?
- That Jesus shed His blood for your sins!?
- That Jesus redeemed you from the curse of the law?
- That Jesus became poor so that you could become rich?
- That God gave you the power to speak life or death into your life?
- That God gave you the power through His Son, Jesus, to come boldly to the throne and make your requests known to Him?
- That God said that you are blessed — both coming in

In Conclusion...

and going out?
- That God gave you goodness and mercy, and He has instructed them to follow you every day for the rest of your life?
- That all things work together for the good of those who love the Lord?
- That Jesus is your advocate and representative before God?
- That faith is the ONLY thing that will move God?
- That if you don't know the answer to any situation in your life, you can ask God for wisdom and understanding, and He will give it to you?

List of the Most Recognized Mothers and Daughters in the Bible

Eve

Sarah

Rebekah

Jochebed

Hannah

Bathsheba

Elizabeth

Mary

Rachel

Eunice

Aquila

Salome

Herodias

Ruth

Naomi

Mary and Martha

Mary Magdalene

Samaritan Woman

Crippled Woman

Adultery Woman

Mother-in-law of Peter's

Widow with Two Mites

Canaanite Woman

Menstruating Woman

In Conclusion...

Widow of Nain
Daughter of Jairus
Mary of Bethany
Persistent Widow
Anna
Joanna
Susanna
Miriam
Lois
Priscilla
Deborah
Tamar
Jezebel
Queen of Sheba
Rahab
Delilah
Abigail
Wife of Lot
Huldah
Gomer
Lydia
Athaliah
Jehosheba
Rizpah
Mical
Jael

DR. BESSIE FLETCHER, PH.D.
Christian Clinical Psychologist, Chaplain and Mother and Daughter Relationship Expert

Dr. Fletcher, (Known as Dr. Bessie) is the Founder and Senior Minister of Mother and Daughter Faith Trust Ministries, www.mdbn.org Dr. Bessie has successfully coached thousands of mothers and daughters to achieve their "Best" relationships, by changing their "Intra-Conversations."

In addition to being a Chaplain and a Christian Clinical Psychologist, Dr. Bessie is an Author of three books, (Dream Recipe, Seventy X Seven and Good News: God Speaks to Mothers and Daughters) Radio Host of the Mother and Daughter Roundtable (broadcasting live weekly every Saturday on Blogtalkradio.com), Publisher of the Mother and Daughter Bonding Magazine, whose cover has featured the First Lady

Michelle Obama.

Dr. Bessie holds a Bachelor of Science degree in Psychology, a Master's in Community Economic Development, a Ph.D. in Christian Clinical Psychology, Post Master's studies in Human Resource and Counseling, a Theological Degree, as an Ordained Pastor/Chaplain.

Dr. Bessie is a powerful, Global renowned Lecturer, Corporate and Personal Development Trainer, Spiritual Teacher and Motivational Speaker who have lectured, trained and motivated individuals from public housing residents, churches, community based organizations, as well as, Fortune 500 Corporations, (AT&T, HUD, Department of Human Resource, American Institution Of Banking, Barnes and Nobles), and others throughout the U.S. and abroad since 1988.

But, she is best known as, The Mother and Daughter Bonding Relationship Expert!

www.ingramcontent.com/pod-product-compliance
Lightning Source LLC
Chambersburg PA
CBHW070617300426
44113CB00010B/1566

* 9 7 8 0 9 9 1 6 5 1 5 5 9 *